HOW TO SPOT
A PRINCE & MARRY
MR RIGHT

THE WEDDING
FAIRY

How to Spot a Prince and Marry Mr Right
published in 2016 by
Acorn Books
www.acornbooks.co.uk

Typography and layout by
Andrews UK Limited
www.andrewsuk.com

George Watts

Contents

A Little Bit About Me

Better known as *The Wedding Fairy,* I am flattered to be considered a leading voice on everything linked to the World of Saying *I do* and have worked in the business of making big day dreams a reality for nearly a decade. From the cake to the dress and everything in between, I am the wedding obsessive, who refuses to accept anything less than utterly spectacular when planning a celebration to remember. Whether it be dripping in diamante, or riddled in glitz 'n' glamour, any wedding is my kind of wedding – no matter how big or small – because at the heart of it all (when you strip away the superficial glitz), you'll find the most precious gift life itself can offer... love. It's the one thing money can't buy and in most circumstances, when you're in it, it really is all we need.

I am often asked what I imagine my own wedding day to be like and in my line of work it is clearly something I have planned out to precision. Liza Minnelli flying in on a zip wire gives you some idea on the kind of scale I am thinking! All I need to do now is find a willing volunteer/victim to make it all happen. I should take a leaf out of my own book right? In many ways it actually feels like I have written this book as a blueprint just for myself. We all tend to be great at offering advice to others when it comes to relationships, but ignore what is blatantly staring us in the face for ourselves. Taking the time to stop and think tends to unlock so much in our heads that we already knew without ever realising, it's just a case of listening to it – something I intend to do a lot more of in the future. Having spent nearly 3 years observing, researching and studying relationships, I almost feel like an 'expert' in this field – although I am not sure anybody ever really becomes such a thing with regards to this subject matter. Isn't it a 'work in progress' for us all? That's most definitely how I feel right now, it is a work in progress and I guess that kind of answers the question as to why I took on this project in the first place.

So for the very first time (with all the relevant health & safety warnings issued and checks in place), I am being let loose on the World of dating and I must admit I am quietly rather excited about the carnage about to ensue. What if this actually works and I get to plan a wedding I made happen? The internal hysteria at such a possibility is almost unbearable for me to control. But why even bother trying to play cupid in the first place I hear you cry? Am I not content being knee-deep in chiffon and Swarovski on an average working day? Well of course I am who wouldn't be? Wedding planning is probably the greatest job of all, but the burdening task of helping others find love just wouldn't go away. It suddenly became all consuming and something I simply couldn't ignore. You see a shift in destiny occurred whilst sipping a skinny cappuccino and chomping on a nut infused biscotti in a cafe with a close friend. Hard as nails it was too, nearly took half my teeth out. Anyway I digress, the point is, it was during a general conversation about dating that I suddenly realised I had way too much to say on the subject matter and that it would just be plain rude of me not to share. Yes fate does indeed move in mysterious ways, and there it was, my eureka moment and thus this book was born. Even the title spontaneously tripped off the tongue in that coffee shop. And trust me that was no easy feat battling with 'that' biscotti.

Just like that, in the flash of an instant, my calling cards were delivered and I am now officially playing matchmaker. Who would've thought it? A natural gravitation some might say, or the perfect role for somebody who has seen it all whilst working in the world of weddings? I adore observing people, their interactions and finding out their business, so either way, writing this book is a dream come true. I am inquisitive by nature, so team this with my unique insight on a day to day basis of observing the very best and worst a relationship has to offer and I may well have bagged a winning formula for success! For me personally, that is a hugely exciting possibility.

Yes some may try to argue that my study is unfounded, even weak, lacking in academic back-up and laced with unproven theories. Shocking words I know. Pure lies, deceit and treachery the lot of it, for my strategy is based upon the observations of life and no amount of theory can trump that card. Don't believe a vile word they say. Soak up these wise words girlfriend, I may just be about to change your life forever... and so, as we set sail, I hope you find this read enlightening, inspiring, thought-provoking, empowering, motivating and most of all bloody hilarious.

Enjoy the ride – no pun intended.
George xx

For more from George, visit theweddingfairy.tv **or connect via FB/Twitter:** WeddingFairyUK

A girl who fails to prepare, is prepared to fail...

(Based on an original quote by Benjamin Franklin)

HOW TO SPOT
A PRINCE & MARRY
MR RIGHT

Part One

Starting the Search

Once Upon a Fairytale

At this precise moment in time as you are about to tuck into this read, it will probably feel utterly impossible to comprehend, but – believe it or not – there was a time when you actually thought a bloke was potentially half decent. I know it sounds ridiculous, but trust me, at some point or another we have all met a match that was perfectly pleasant and at the very least had a glimmer of potential. Quite clearly I am not talking about the inappropriate propositions one has had to endure, whilst a vile creature has been masticating on a garlic mayonnaise drenched doner kebab, post being swept out with the bottles of one's local nightspot – the mental image alone makes me feel violently sick and that's before we even begin to think about the gut wrenching stench. I am of course referring to those guys that actually seemed vaguely normal.

So before we kick off this life-changing project, take a moment to reflect on your back catalogue – of men that is not Beyonce hit's you've downloaded – and consider what positive qualities attracted you to your favourites in the first place. Bank those thoughts and ditch the rest. I say 'positive' in the sense that we are now looking for a keeper, not a one night wonder. And yes I do know that the latter can be a little addictive, but this is a cut throat mission lady and we have no time for chewing the fat over some no hope maybe, or a gansta bad boy that is clearly going to take you no further than a Nando's on any given Saturday night out. These guys are officially dead to you. Now is the time for hunting out a suitor for life not just for Christmas. Think delicate debutante not drunk and desperate.

Talking of debutantes (defined as an upper-class young woman making her first appearance in fashionable society), there is actually much to be said for some cultures that have perfected the calculated art of match-making and it shouldn't be instantly dismissed. I have witnessed the success first hand of a well executed arranged relationship. After all, organising a blind date between two people is simply based on judgement and isn't so dissimilar in our modern world. The idea of bringing together two people we are sure will 'click', is alive and well in every society across the globe today. I am clearly not talking about anything forced here, and to be fair, the debutante ball is taking things a little too far – thanks to its sexist conveyor belt existence – but borrowing the odd positive point from certain theories that have proven success rates is never a bad thing. I know I am ultimately outing myself for utilising a little established strategy here and there, but having whipped it all up into my own unique formula, I am pretty confident my modern girls guide to finding Mr Right will hit the spot and save on heartache in the long run, not to mention the investment of your valuable time. The dating game can be relentless on that front.

Trolling through the dregs of society can become a seriously disheartening process – especially when the light at the end of the tunnel appears to be totally non-existent. Indeed, non-voluntary celibacy can seem like the only logical way forward and understandably so. At the end of the day, there are only so many frogs you can kiss before one reaches a point of total hysteria. Where the hell is my Prince I hear you cry? And who could blame you. It's moments like these that can drive a girl to drink and we all know how that ends up. Generally face down in a stranger's semi-detached. And thus follows the walk of shame and hence a cycle of despair continues… if you let it!

I know I am being a little heavy handed on the drama front here. What's the harm in a bit of fun between friends after a Saturday night out? The answer of course is absolutely nothing. Good on you girl, I am all for the fun 'n' frolics life has to offer. No-one likes a frigid, but when it comes to settling down, well, the World is full of loser's and I refuse for you to settle with any of them – hence why we need to distinguish Prince from pauper. Like I need to tell you that right? I bet you've met a few of the latter in your time. The fact he can string a sentence together and seems semi-decent obviously isn't a good thing. And lady, let me remind you, second best just isn't an option in this game going forward. It's incredibly easy to go down that road even though deep down inside we all know it is the wrong option and probably the reason why so many relationships fail in the long term. Settling for anything in life is never a good thing. If you start regularly referring to the fact he is a kind man and treats you well three months in, it's definitely time to walk – especially if that's as far as your feelings go.

I bet as a child, when first hearing the story of Cinders, you dreamt up a version of your very own Prince Charming in your head right? It is without doubt one of those pinnacle moments, when a little girl begins to mentally structure their ideal for a future partner. And in my opinion those early visions should not be dismissed. Quite often in life, the first thought is the best thought – at any age – so why settle for anything less? Why not work on shaping a reality you've always dreamt of – ok, maybe from an imaginative early childhood is pushing it a bit, but you get the idea. It may take a little determination and persistence, but the power is now well and truly in your hands to shape your future. Think the unthinkable girlfriend because it's time to reach for new highs! The only people to ever hold us back in life are generally ourselves. Ok so in reality, you may have to re-adjust some of the visual expectations and fine tune a few characteristics here and there, but hey – what's life without a challenge. Even the finest of the male specimen needs a spot of re-moulding every now and then to extract the perfect gent. The important point is to recognise a Prince Charming potential and it's my personal quest and mission to show you how.

Now as I have already stated, many may decide to mock my little book as a superficial and vacuous vessel in attempting to find Mr Right. Well, I beg to differ. Look below the surface and you will find heart and soul that will ultimately spark a victorious voyage to the aisle of 'I do'. But before we set sail with any of that, it's also important I turn my attention on to you, so we can knock out any lingering fears of self-doubt and pop into check mate position. It can be a little unnerving putting yourself 'out there', but trust me, there really is no need to morph into a panicking wreck at this junction, simply grab that bull by the horns so to speak and go with the flow girl – it's time to get this party started. What's the worst that could happen anyhow? Nobody really cares that much, or actually notices those things in life we are super conscious about, or have insecurities over that often hold us back – so why let them? Take this journey with me and I promise, no more shall you need to dine-in on a solo sweaty boil in the bag, for you my lady deserve a table for two and that's a fact. Say bon-voyage to that soul destroying ready meal for one... the cod to your chips is out there somewhere – all we need to do is track and trace.

But for all the positivity and words of wisdom I or anyone else can offer, destiny doesn't always land in our laps. Sometimes we have to hunt it down for ourselves and actions always speak louder than words. Living your life through a series of natural expectations is a dangerous thing anyhow and often leads to disappointment. The fact you have picked up this book in the first place suggests you are now ready to go forth and start in your search to bag a Prince, but light hearted efforts need not apply. This task needs your full attention going forward, whilst the rest of your life takes a backseat for a while. I repeat half hearted attempts need not apply. No more running, no more hiding and no more excuses. This is it.

Of course we all know that true love and a soul-mate to share your life with conquers all, but perseverance – not luck – is often the name of the game in the beginning. No offence, but all your friends are SO totally bored of the same old clichéd conversations about not being able to find the man of your dreams bla bla bla and who could blame them. No-one wants to be friends with a desperado who is no good to man or feral beast. Ok, so maybe they have already bagged themselves a hot hunk, which makes the whole thing slightly sickening I grant you, but screw them and focus on you. No more moaning, or woe is me moments – now is the time for action.

Get yourself in the zone girlfriend. Are you ready for this challenge and I mean really ready? Because sometimes in life we say we really want something, but actually, in reality, we aren't necessarily all that bothered. Or more likely, have been subconsciously avoiding the challenge for some reason. When you actually stop and really think about it, has there been some kind of barrier holding you back personally, that needs to be overcome, before you can fully commit to this process? Stop and seriously think about these questions carefully because they need answering and resolving before you can move forward successfully. I know it kind of sounds ridiculous, but you will be surprised how much a fear for the unknown, or a lack of confidence for example can be massively restricting. It's time to get focused and into the right headspace, because part of this process being successful is reliant on you and your approach to it.

Now my book could come across as a little anti-man at times, but I promise you it's not an overriding thought of mine. It's something I have been acutely aware of and tried very hard not to do too much of. But I guess this read is precautionary by nature because I am constantly referring to all the negatives you need to look out for and what to avoid. Sadly in most circumstances that list is a lot longer than the other! Add in the fact I am also trying to highlight what isn't right, won't work and what to ignore – it can at times all come across as a little 'anti'. I don't mean it too, which is why it's important for me to highlight at this junction, but in many ways also sums up the approach you should take in finding Mr Right in the first place – never ignore the warning signs and always let your gut feelings guide you. It's a bit like when you ponder over a potential internet date you are not sure about going on because that all important 'gut feeling' keeps getting in the way. Was it ever wrong? I doubt it. If a bond is not feeling right you will soon know about it and that also applies when you haven't even met it seems!

And finally whatever you do, never forget that men really are very simple creatures with a limited thought process and a minimal attention span – I should know I am one! Remember that and you are set up for life. The bottom line is, they will never make sense to you, accept that and you are half way there and on to a winner... what was I saying about being anti-men?!

A man who knows what he wants is the only type worth knowing...

Talking Tactics

Get ready to unleash your inner Panther lady, as we prepare for attack and lay the bait to reel-in your prey of choice. From this point forward, bagging a Prince is absolutely your number one priority. As I said, it's time to hit that pause button and momentarily pop the rest of your life on hold. If you are truly determined to bag a keeper, the task ahead demands your complete focus and full attention. Half hearted attempts just won't cut it I am afraid – otherwise the only journey you'll be taking is a one-way ticket to *Singlesville* – population one, and that certainly isn't the booking I have in mind for you sweet cheeks.

Prepping for a Prince is certainly a time consuming affair, but an effort I guarantee will be worth it in the long run. As with anything in life, the more you put in, the more you get out. Are you ready for action? I say that, because right from the word go, you need be feeling good both inside and out to make this happen. And that doesn't mean you have to hit the gym hard or undergo a major makeover to secure a winner – although for many this can be a great confidence booster – you just need to be comfortable in your own skin. And whatever that means for you, it's important to get to a point of feeling at ease about yourself so you can really move forward with the challenge ahead. I always say, extract all the bits you are happy with and dump the rest. Why bother focusing on the negative when it always feels so much better to concentrate on the positive? Lock out the former because if you don't love yourself a little how on earth can you expect someone else too?

Stepping up to the challenge of proactively hunting out a man requires nerves of steel, skin as thick as a rhino and a solid state of mind. Shake out any negativity and force yourself into a zone of positivity at all times. The mind can be a difficult beast to tame, but tell yourself something often enough and you will start to believe it. Personal confidence can be a barrier in so many parts of our lives – especially where relationships are concerned. Even from a young age, one's confidence can take a bit of a battering without even realising it. Still to this day, I cannot believe teachers used to tell me I smiled too much? Talk about trying to stunt a child's spirit! The best one was a teacher who told my parent's, 'I was too happy in the classroom'. Really?! And that's before we even begin to consider careers, social interactions and the dreaded ageing process... blimey I think I'll stop myself there before we all want to jump off the roof and end it all! This is an inspiring and uplifting read I promise. My point is that over time, all those little knocks can make an impact, but those knocks can also be easily manipulated and moulded into making you a stronger person if you let them. After all, a lady that perseveres with anything in life will never fail. And that includes your mindset.

Of course at the other end of the scale, you may be feeling quietly confident and have no idea why the man of your dreams hasn't landed in your lap yet? You've possibly reached a point of feeling like there have been a million chances with date after date going nowhere and it's just not meant to be. Fate has dealt its cards and you were born to be a happy spinster with only a furry friend for company. Quite often this sort of mindset leads to an acceptance with 'your lot' and that is a very dangerous place to be too. At worst, you stop caring altogether and stop being bothered about making any real effort – lacklustre at best. If that is the case, thank goodness you picked up this book! Men can sniff out all of the above in an instant and they don't like it. They need to know you care and haven't given up on the L word. Contentment can seriously stifle your productivity in finding Mr Right. Yes life might be good right now and it's only the cherry on top that is missing, but quite often it's the final piece of the jigsaw that makes the biggest impact.

Identify where your head is at right now and reboot as needed. A moment's reflection for a spot of fine tuning never did anyone any harm. Self analysis can be hugely uncomfortable, but is often the only way we can make a shift in our behavioural patterns and thought processes for the better. Nine times out of ten, it's just a case of having a bit of a word with ourselves to get things back on track. Realign those chakras girlfriend we need a positive energy flow going on! Who knows, your Mr Right may be just around the corner, or even standing next to you on the rush hour commute home this eve. And if that's the case, we need you feeling good from the inside out post haste. No opportunity for interaction should be missed. Practice makes perfect after all. As of now, we are officially wiping the slate clean and re-launching you back onto the dating scene.

Walking with my eyes wide open is a mantra I live by. None of us can predict the future, but if you're open to possibilities, the next day kick starts a whole new adventure. And that pretty much sums up exactly what this process is – an adventure. If you feel like you are on lockdown right now – as in, stop no entry, don't cross over the line – now is the time to activate a fresh start. Nobody wants to make an effort with the miserable cow sat in the corner with nothing to say for herself. Little is less attractive. An enthusiasm and zest for life is what we are after. All of us are naturally drawn to a positive energy. It's the absolute best way to bag a bloke. And if you're not feeling it right now – fake it! The feel-good vibe will rub off on you eventually. Just remember, the look we are going for is alive, alert and interested. Open to conversation and keen to chat, with an undercurrent of being available – but not over cooking it on the enthusiasm front. There is of course a fine line and having a protective guard up – not too high of course – is never a bad thing when entering the world of dating.

Most guys like to lead an initial encounter and tend to pull out all the stops to impress. Simply step back, observe, even judge a little and let them crack on. Give him your undivided and uninterrupted attention. Immerse yourself in the conversation if you feel like he's worth a punt. Men need to know that they have a fighting chance after all. In the same vein, no-one likes a quitter, so he must also demonstrate a sense of perseverance to show he means business. It's a tricky balancing act this dating malarkey, but ultimately all guys love a little testing in the first instance.

The big question of course, is how do we get to this point? And by that I mean the initial encounter – not to be confused with brief – this is clearly the bit most people struggle with. Where the hell do you find this perfect bloke I keep chatting about? We will come on to those specifics in a moment. But before we delve into such waters, we must also consider strategy. And before any initial encounter can commence, there must be an initial hunt and that's the important bit to be prepared for. From this point forward, you need to have your wits about you and be at the ready for any potential hunt you may encounter. Never tell yourself that a guy is just being friendly or 'nice' if he is single and tries to talk with you. Gosh I hate that word. As an English teacher once told me, 'never use the word nice', it's so offensive. Nothing should ever be nice. It's so middle-of-the-road verging upon insipid. Dating should never be nice either. When a girlfriend tells me she had a nice time, I always tell her to dump him. Anyway I digress (again), a boy is blatantly chatting you up if he pop's over for a little chat. Let's face it, he's not trying to make a new friend my love, this is a strategic move on his part. Go with it. Who knows, you might strike up a bit of a connection and if not, it's always good to dip said toe in the water at any given opportunity.

I must also stress that when I say *the initial hunt,* I refer to your good self as the hunted not the hunter. No man on Earth can bear a psychotic female pacing the bar like a caged animal, desperately searching for anything with a pulse. Men are like a pack of wolves, they can sniff out desperation from a mile away and I can assure you it ain't no aphrodisiac. The male species is essentially a feral beast and loves nothing more than the chase. A little light flirty eye contact is never a bad thing, as is being attentive, but transforming into a hysterical giggling mess is never a good look. Just be you and keep those nerves in check by telling your head what to do whilst your heart freestyles. I am not saying play it total cold bitch, but I am saying act a little aloof, whilst retaining a mildly sassy nature. And always ensure the conversation is open-ended. Ultimately it is the hunter's job to sweep you off your feet and not the other way round, but at the same time don't slam that door shut before he has even got started.

Now as we speak, I can already hear a rally of feminist cries and the equality banners being erected below my balcony, but you cannot argue with nature people. The facts are there for all to see. Survey 100 people and I bet the most successful relationships have all started with the man playing hunter. And by that I am not saying he is 'Lord and Master' before the banners come out again. I am simply pointing out that in the first instance a man loves to chase – it's a testosterone thing. And it's a massive turn on for him, so for everyone's sake, let him get it all out and over with at the earliest opportunity, saves all manner of problems further down the line. Unleash the beast and let it run free as they say. The future dynamic of a relationship and how it is shaped is ultimately down to you anyhow. In reality, this has never really been a man's World has it? The female species after all is his biggest addiction.

Right moving forward we need to also consider the rules of engagement and avenues for said hunt. I have spoken a lot already about opening up barriers, but that isn't just from an emotional perspective. You need to get yourself to a point whereby you really want to grab this adventure by the balls and try out new things. And I don't mean sexually by the way! I simply refer to the fact that you must put yourself out there and make yourself available for said hunt. Nobody is going to find you wrapped up on the sofa watching back to back Corrie and Eastenders with a milky Milo are they?!

Getting the mind-set in check is absolutely vital during these early stages, so ditch any anxieties you have built up about bagging the one and embrace the thrill of entering unknown territories. And the first step in your quest is to tell anyone and everyone who will listen that you are officially on a mission to find Mr Right! Even some fun posts via social media, having a bit of a giggle about the fact you are single and ready to mingle, or heading out on a 'singles night' for example, are all good moves. Be loud, proud and bold. There is nothing to be ashamed of here. Someone might know someone who they think you could be a great match with and one social media post could be the spark of something special. No opportunity should be missed. Encourage friends to set you up on a blind date for a laugh, or manipulate an intro with a colleague they know and think could be suitable for example.

Go traditional and organise a night out on the razzle-dazzle. Believe it or not, people do still meet in bars and nightclubs! Of course, it's also important to take advantage of the online dating scene. Sign up to a website and get yourself out there girl. Focus on one website/app at a time so as not to overwhelm yourself. If you feel it's not working for you at first, don't give up, simply move on and try out a new site. There are so many options available right now and everyday there is a new star on the scene. My advice would be to hit a search engine such as Google and search under 'best dating apps/website' for a current list of the hottest contenders. Make sure you invest and take time in preparing your profile too. Select a good mix of pictures and don't worry, you are not alone when it comes to the torturous 'about me' section. Most people struggle, so why not get a friend on board to help you with this part of the process. It can actually be quite a giggle over a glass of bubbles and a box of choccies. It's also ok to 'like' someone and ignite an interaction. Don't just wait around to be found online. I know in a way this is at odds with my earlier words on the man playing hunter, but that doesn't mean you have to simply sit back and wait for the man of your dreams to land on your laptop. This is a proactive move that will ignite the hunt. Sometimes a guy needs a little shove in the right direction – nothing wrong with that.

Dating agencies either online or locally shouldn't be dismissed either. Yes, the classic match-making service that arranges introductions on behalf of people searching for love has actually made quite a resurgence because let's face it, if a guy is prepared to invest a decent amount of hard cold cash for an agency to match him up with a potential suitor then clearly he means business. And anyway, some online dating sites or apps – especially the free ones with thousands of members – can start to feel a bit like a conveyor belt existence with all that swiping left or right, proving quite disheartening and unproductive after a while. Certainly get involved and give every potential route to love a go, the simple moral of the story here is to try out lot's of routes to success not just stick to one.

Entering new environments such as joining a community group or taking up a socially interactive hobby are all great ways to meet new people as well. Perhaps you have a particular interest you have always wanted to explore further? Now is the time to do it. Don't put off today what you can do tomorrow as they say. Get online and take a look at what is happening in your local area and get involved. I once encouraged a friend to join the local WI group and she bagged a marriage out of that one. All organised in seconds via a friend of a friend at a social gathering... they are going great guns right now!

In a way, it's about widening your social reach, not restricting it with the same circle of friends, repeating the same activities over and over again. Step outside the box. Book and film clubs for example are becoming very popular and often prove to be hugely social. As are sporting groups. And don't forget the classic 'works do' or being on-guard during professional networking events either. I would never encourage an office romance for logistical reasons, but a few drinks with the girls after work is always a great way to get interacting with a potential Prince who might catch your eye. Look out for events locally that offer an opportunity to socialise too. Drag a friend along with you in the first instance – ideal if they are also single – but don't stay locked to each other all evening!

I haven't ever heard any long-term success stories through 'speed dating' nights, but who knows, it might prove to be a bit of fun for a night out. At this point it's all about *putting yourself out there* and not taking the whole thing too seriously. Sod it, why not book a week away with the girls… grab that bottle of mateus rose; we are heading for the Algarve girl. Love in the sun, here we come! Jokes aside, whatever or however you decide to kick start the new you – because in a way that is what we are talking about here – just always remember to stay safe, meet people in a public place and never go off alone with anyone until you feel completely comfortable in their company. Always tell a friend where the date is taking place too.

Sometimes in life you just have to ditch rationality and action all those things you have wanted to do, but have been putting off for whatever reason. Re-launch the new you with a bit of an adventure. What's stopping you? Make it happen. Money and time are all excuses. Liberate and embrace *you* before beginning to think about anyone else. After all, this is the key to being hunted in the first place. Non-verbal communication is the most powerful of all our sexual senses and a lady that oozes confidence both inside and out, is the ultimate turn on for any man. Being comfortable in one's skin is the only option. Let go of any negativities you feel might be holding you back – or indeed a general laziness towards the whole thing too! Shake it out girl because such energies can easily creep in without us even realising. It doesn't always need to be a deep and meaningful block. Sometimes we just give up and can't be arsed. Get back on the horse girl. Quite often, the barrier to finding Mr Right is down to our own actions, or lack of.

And remember, practice makes perfect! If at first you don't succeed, try and try again. Don't give up at the first hurdle. Online dating can be especially relentless and does take some serious commitment and perseverance. I have a friend who went on twenty dates before she met 'the one'! But I guess in a way, that is the magic of searching digitally – you can test run a whole mix of models you might not necessarily have considered before. It's a bit like trying on a wedding dress for the first time. You may be pretty confident you know your own style, but it's often the least favourite dress on the hanger you fall in love with. Online dating can be very similar and is often full of surprises. The amount of people that tell me they have fallen for someone via a match-making website who isn't their normal type is quite staggering. Don't stifle your options, try out a whole mix of potential suitors and see what clicks.

All too often in life we build barriers and limit our options, but this entire process is about freeing up all the red tape we create for ourselves on a daily basis and re-activating the idea that anything is possible. I guess it's an age thing really. The older we get the more set in our ways we become. But that is never a good move. Be prepared to put yourself out there and open to the possibility of trying out new things. It might not be so easy at first, but once you find your feet, I promise you will uncover an inner confidence you never knew existed.

As I have already said and cannot overstate enough, you are not going to find Mr Right parked on the sofa every night watching back to back soaps. A Monday night soap-a-thon being the only exception I will allow! Personally I love nothing more than watching 2.5 hours of our Nation's favourites back to back at the start of a working week, in my leopard print dressing gown, whilst chomping on an almond magnum. But when it turns into a nightly occurrence, slap yourself and get out of the house. Even if it's just to take the dog for a walk… and before you say it, if you don't own one, offer to take the neighbours for a walk. Who knows, you might even meet the man of your dreams whilst bagging a doggy doo doo?! In fact, you don't even need a dog, go for a walk in the park and strike up a conversation. Obviously not in a dogging slash cottaging type way… actually on second thoughts, I am getting myself into doggy – I mean – dodgy water here, maybe start with the local coffee shop and go from there!

And I am not just talking about finding a man here. I refer to life in general. I have a friend who set herself the personal challenge of striking up a conversation with two new people every day for a month. In many ways, I think it was a bit of a kick up the arse she was looking for and this proved a fun way to step outside of her daily routine that was getting her down a bit. And yes I know it does sound a bit cringe – especially if you are not hugely confident – but I watched in awe as this person went from strength to strength, observing some of the amazing conversations that were had. Honestly it was incredible to watch. Of course, not everyone was receptive, but she persevered and that of course is all part of the challenge. But the moment she really hit it off with a random and engaged in a meaningful conversation, well, it really did boost her confidence no end. From that point on, nothing was going to stop her. Its amazing how one little challenge can trigger such determination and quite often so many life changes … she got a date about two weeks in and the rest as they say is history.

I know most of what we have spoken about thus far is more to do with what's going on internally more than your actions externally, but I do also think it's a good idea to rock a bit of a makeover every now and then. You just can't beat a spot of feel-good superficiality in my opinion! And anyway joking aside, I really do believe that feeling good on the outside also impacts on our mental well-being on the inside. Being comfortable in your own skin is utterly vital for long-term happiness and in many ways your future relationship. You may be questioning at this juncture what all this has to do with finding Mr Right – well it has everything to do with finding Mr Right. At the heart of all my tactics for spotting a Prince is you and how you feel. Positive clearly being the ideal outcome! Of course, we are never going to love every element of our physical self, but learning to accept our lot is really important not only when dating, but in life too.

Right, let's have some fun lady! First up it's time to re-fresh that wardrobe. Out with the old and in with the new as they say. And don't be afraid of adding a little sparkle here and there either. A dash of diamante never did anyone any harm. I will have you dressed up like a Drag Queen in no time if we carry on like this! Again I am SO totally joking, but I do personally always find a little de-clutter a rather cathartic experience and the best remedy for initiating a fresh start. And whilst you're at it, book that appointment for a restyle at the local hair salon you have been meaning to do for a while too. And I am sorry, but a plain-Jane-no-nonsense trim is totally out the window. Be experimental, there's nothing worse than getting stuck in your ways on the follicle front. Next up, if you are keen to knock off a couple of pounds, why not also take this opportunity to activate an action plan. Kate Moss once said, 'Nothing tastes as good as skinny feels'. A sentiment that really struck me and although I certainly don't think you need to be skinny to be gorgeous, a little body toning can be a miracle worker in maxing your curves and highlighting your sexy bits. Finally, top this lot off with a visit to your local department store for a free make-up and make-over consultation… I can feel a new you evolving as we speak!

Now as we sign off on this chapter, on occasion, logistics, fate, or a mixture of the two, can get in the way of my traditional strategies for said 'hunt' and therefore we must sometimes break rank and ditch said rules of engagement. And although a little nervous about such a recommendation, I am at heart a rule breaker. Yes, I am of course referring to an *immediate impact*. An inappropriate moment for interaction, but an opportunity not to be missed. I can feel that pulse rate rising as we speak! An immediate impact is beyond exciting. In fact it's my favourite kind of meet and even though it's not a regular situation one will have to face, it's always best to be on guard. For example, you might find yourself knee deep in a coffee shop business meeting, sipping on a cappuccino, whilst intensely chewing the fat over figures, when a Prince suddenly strikes. Quite clearly this is an inappropriate time for any man to interrupt a lady at work. How on earth could a real gent ignite the hunt uninvited and under such circumstances? Especially if you haven't even made eye contact or you simply decide to ignore the situation. Both bad moves by the way if you like what you see! Look, if you hit the jackpot and a real Prince Charming with balls of steel zips over to leave a business card without a signal on your part, I would ditch the figures and run for your life – that man is clearly a keeper lady. In reality of course, this is highly unlikely to happen and therefore it is down to you to manage the situation.

And the key to making an immediate impact work for you is my 'mirror, signal, manoeuvre' formula. Give him a bit of a visual that you are indeed happy to be hunted and a signal that he is indeed welcome to pop over to your table. A few simple glances and a cheeky smile should do the trick! No need to over play it. Enthusiastically legging it over to the bar in a vain attempt to catch his attention whilst stacking it half way en route, is again no winning look. Under no circumstances must you go up and speak to him. I will totally die if you do. Such a move is way to ballsy for an initial meet and will unease the hunter. The moment is then lost forever. As I say, this is a simple mirror, signal and strategic manoeuvre situ. It's now in the hands of fate as to whether he decides to make his move and you are meant to be joined together in Holy Matrimony. And if he does or has, well congratulations, you may well have already bagged the man of your dreams in the last 24 hours… if not keep reading!

The First Flutter of Hope

Let's not beat about the bush here ladies, that first flutter for anyone persevering with the dating game is really quite a moment. And happen it will if you keep persevering. It reminds us that the L word is worth fighting for. In that very instant, one's eyes are once again wide open to the possibility of finding love. And the best bit is that you only need to feel it once to reignite those sexual senses that have been void of attention for far too long. Yes a little effort is required to succeed in what can often feel like a battle one has no chance of winning. But recharged those batteries will be, if you commit to the tactics and don't give up at the first hurdle.

Most importantly of course, the first flutter will give you hope. It's very easy to forget what a sensational feeling we are dealing with here and all too easy to reside yourself to a life of singledom. As I say, the amount of people I meet who tell me that relationship's just don't seem to work for them is quite unbelievable. Yes, at times it can feel like a relentless struggle, but hope is the ultimate antidote in spurring yourself along in this quest to find a partner. Reaching the point of hope certainly requires much effort on your part – especially if you're having to hunt for love and Mr Right doesn't just land in your lap – but total focus and dedication to my tactics will deliver the desired results. Nothing ever comes to those who wait in the wings remember.

Of course if you haven't sampled the goods for some time, it's very easy to let go of hope all together and drift off into no man's land. When it comes to sex, if you don't bother having any, one can easily forget how bloody marvellous it can be. Simply feeling desired is an aphrodisiac in itself let alone anything physical, and let's face it nothing beats a spot of good old fashioned flattery for a positivity kick either. Letting go of hope in the first place is often where the problems start and is definitely not an option in the dating game. Before you know it, you become too scared to chase a happy ever after and that's when the darkness sets in. And yes, you might just experience a second rate tingle upon re-launch, but who cares. Hope has been reignited and that official first flutter is within easy reach…

I am not going to mince my words here ladies. Pre, post or during that life changing moment when your eyes first meet and click with a potential keeper – and mark my words they will click if you keep trying – one should experience a sensational sensation deep within that makes you wanna throw your arms up in the air like you just don't care. A sizzling shockwave that runs through the body telling you that something rather special is happening. To be honest, I am truly hysterical just thinking about your first flutter. It will be a moment to cherish, for the charming Prince of your dreams could be standing right in front of you any day now. And trust me, it will happen and when it strikes – you will know about it! It might take a few kick-starts in the beginning, but I have absolute confidence it will happen.

The idea that two people meet and have the capability to connect on such a level is just incredible to me. Human instinct, interaction and sexual connection is both baffling and fascinating – a book in itself some might say. But for me, this is what the first flutter is all about. A prelude to the real deal and although many will disagree, it all starts with the visuals. If honest with ourselves, it's what we need to be drawn to in the first place right? All too often I hear people harping on about the importance of personality and looks not being so important, but this hype is a simple pr exercise by certain individuals trying to convince themselves that they are happy in a second rate love nest. Looks are not just important when it comes to sexual attraction they are essential and all in the eye of the beholder. Sexual chemistry is what binds a relationship together; otherwise you may as well just be good mates. The clicking of personalities is of course a vital ingredient in sealing something truly special, but it's the physical attraction that kick's-in to allow for that possibility in the first place. Ok in some circumstances a guy could turn out to be utterly gorgeous but a total social hand grenade. That would be pretty unfortunate and bad luck all round because let's face it, a personality that grates is never going to be something we can just learn to live with. Even if he is super hot! Looks fade, personalities are eternal, but in the first instance it really is all about the visuals.

Breaking it down, if you don't stop and think 'phwoah he's proper lush' – ditch there and then. And yes some might say I am being a little fickle here, but what's the point in banging your head against a brick wall people? I am just trying to save you a whole load of wasted effort and emotional upheaval here girls. If the visuals are not on par and he doesn't make you feel a little giddy on the inside, it's time to do a Craig David and walk away. We don't have time for the 'perhaps we could give it a try' conversation. Conviction to the cause of bagging a Prince is all that matters. Screw maybe's and definitely chuck potentials out the window. I am only interested in finding the one that rocks your world with a first flutter so bad, it could knock you to the ground. Within that first blink of an eye, both head and beating heart will know if this boy is hot to trot into your life – or at the very least – worth a shot.

Generally in life, we learn our lessons the hard way, and when it comes to men, I am sure you've had your fingers burnt once or twice in the past. And yes, it is possible your first flutter won't necessarily be a keeper, but that doesn't matter, it's a great boost to experience such an interaction and will drive you forward wanting more. Let your hair down and have a little fun – you're single so flirt away! And on that note, screw any rejection that a guy might try and throw your way too. If he pulls away that is his problem. Focus on moving forward not on time wasters. One has to become a little emotionally detached, almost ruthless, to truly spot a Prince and Marry Mr Right. And don't bother trying to be friends if things don't work out, especially if he suggests it. It means one of two things. A) He still fancies you, or B) He just wants to sleep with you. Either way, it's not going to work out if you are ready to move on. It is my strong belief that a straight guy and a straight girl cannot ever be good friends in general anyhow, without at least one fancying the other, be it post relationship or not. Such 'friendships' generally end in disaster. Apart from the odd anomaly here and there, I have never been proven wrong.

Remember, a perfect Prince should excite, surprise and quite literally take your breath away. The Richter scale of hysteria level needs to be through the roof. Anything less is just average and who really cares for average? Whether your eyes meet on a train, in a bar, or even at a sexual health clinic – who cares! This is the modern age girls, never let a golden nugget slip through the net and never ever dismiss a full on flutter – whatever the situation. Fully engage and see what occurs… fate can move in mysterious ways, but one thing is sure, individually we also have the power to manage that pathway to our desired destiny and ultimately our happy ever after too.

Now once an actual prime bate potential has been caught and we have a full blown flutter on our hands, it is your job to play it cool, calm and sophisticated to trigger his curiosity and leave a lasting impression he cannot ignore. All men be it Prince or pauper are sexually triggered by intrigue, so it's essential we hit a prime target head on to ignite the chase. I want this man running down the street begging for your number because both head and heart is telling him that fate has brought you together. And yes I am a fatalist at heart, but as I say, sometimes a good egg can accidentally escape the nest, so make sure you grab that heart by the balls and leave him begging for more. Who wants to be left with the 'what could have been' taste in their mouth?

Wise words I know, but every time I reflect on the title of this chapter, it's not the first flutter that really drives me on. I always come back to the power of hope and what an incredible affect that feeling can have when it kicks in. Many aspects of our lives our guided by hope and no other word could be more appropriate at this juncture. Hope for the best as they say. You may have given up on it until now and that's why it is so important to rekindle. Forget all that has past and focus on the future. There's a reason my friends constantly tell me that an infectious positive energy riddles my body from head to toe and here's hoping it's rubbing off on you right now.

Mr Right may be just a few flutters away! And the rest of this book is going to guide you on what to do when it happens. Remember, a first class flutter is all we are interested in. Anything second rate need not apply. We have already spoken about potential routes to ignite the first flutter from mainstream online dating to stepping outside of your comfort zone to try new things and meet new people. The challenge for you now is to go make it all happen. Put together an action plan and make a list of all the potential routes and activities that could work for you. As I say, challenge yourself. Get researching, get thinking and get doing. As of now the power really is in your hands.

Part Two

Identifying a Potential Prince

The Aftermath of a First Flutter

Once you have been suitably fluttered or flustered as the case may be, we are ready to move on to what I phrase *the post show analysis*. And if it hasn't happened in the time you turned the page from the last chapter – just imagine it has now! Spark that imagination of yours by drifting off in to a land of hope and utilise those GCSE Drama skills you never thought there would be a use for. Use past potentials as case study's to work from if all else fails! From the first meet, to preparing for the aisle of 'I do', this book is about visualising your entire journey. Positivity breeds positivity and by the way, I have purposely titled this chapter with the word *aftermath* because following a first meet of any significance, there really should be one. Did the chunk of a hunk spark total carnage in both head and heart? Did the initial crescendo of sexual energy ignite an unimaginable desire to find out more about the man who stood before you? Did he leave you speechless wanting more? These are all questions that need to be asked in the aftermath of such a meet. An intense intrigue rarely unearthed should be at the core of any such interaction… I can feel those heart beats arising as I write!

Experiencing such extreme emotions is something us humans tend to develop from an early age. The euphoria of unwrapping ones presents as a child on Christmas day could not be any further from the sinking feeling we experience upon discovering Father Christmas isn't real. A lesson in life some might say, indeed it can be a cruel world, but at the same time you cannot have the highs without the lows, and in many ways it's these moments in our early lives that are an essential part of the process in shaping and evolving our emotional responses. Of course it is those highs we are channelling and focusing on right now – especially the sexual ones post puberty!

And for me it all kicks off with that initial gut instinct. An internal force that is responsible for your first flutter of hope and the intrigue that drives it forward. Never tell yourself what you should be feeling towards somebody because they either seem like a nice guy, or might be a potential over time. In my experience one's gut feeling is rarely wrong and should be trusted much more than any other analytic tool on the market. It's never a good idea to list the pros and cons of an individual either, just go with first impressions. I am of course referring to hardcore raw passion here really, which let's face it, should be at the heart of everything anyhow.

Consider the conversation with a Potential Prince upon first meet also. Did he rock your world with a moment of hilarity or perhaps a sensitive chat that really struck a chord? Cheesy chat up lines need not apply of course – we have all heard enough of those by now right? Non-verbal's are just as important too. Critique every moment of interaction carefully post intro and analyse accordingly. This is your Simon Cowell moment girl. Judge but don't be judged, this bit is about him not you. Is he genuinely the kind of guy you would seriously want to see again and could imagine dating? That's always a good place to start I guess! Never think, 'oh I will just give it a go' because over time committing to such non-starters will dishearten. Keep persevering for the real deal.

Remember actions always speak louder than words too and as such, we need to examine the overall vibe a potential Prince Charming exudes. I don't need to tell you that there is quite a distance between seductive and sleazy, so recognise and examine quickly what a potential beau is hunting for and react accordingly. If he left you dreaming of a first date and how amazing it might well be you could indeed be onto a winner. Are you already thinking long term and that the *Aisle of love* may be just around the corner? It sounds ridiculous I know, but subconsciously all these thoughts gush through our minds like a burst water pipe the minute we meet somebody that matters. A real Mr Right will make you feel like he is fighting for that first date because he can also sense something a little out of the norm from such an unexpected union (wherever it may be) and ultimately that is what will make him stand out from Mr Average and leave you knowing it is potentially something special.

A true Prince will also make you feel at ease and demonstrate he is a man of depth, experience and confidence. A guy you can trust and rely on. He will make you feel secure and protected – all essential ingredients a real Prince amongst men should possess. Because let's face it, can you really be bothered with the hassle of having to fine tune such basics? Of course not and why should you. At the end of the day you want to be his lover not his mother right? If he isn't interesting – ditch. If he doesn't seem interested – ditch. Persistence on his part is an absolute must, as is a desire to impress and woo. Like a dog, a man is for life not just for Christmas so select wisely.

Whether it be a random meet, first date, blind date or an online introduction – the aftermath and its impact is all that matters when considering your next move. And believe it or not, our opinions of another individual and their character are generally subconsciously formed within the first few moments of meeting them. As I say, trust that gut feeling because it's there for a reason. And although over time your opinion may change as you get to know a guy more, that first instinct never really leaves us and is often proved to be right in the long run. In the same vein, try to get a sense of what he is thinking too. Sometimes the chemistry between two people can be so overwhelming that it's difficult to register a rational thought process. Lust can often overtake everything upon a real first flutter. So if not initially, certainly gage his actions wisely as you move into a dating situ, as this is the time for (mildly) rational thinking. Cautionary steps also play their part in guiding us all to a happy ever after.

Spotting the Characteristics of a Keeper

The real drama is always in the detail – especially where men are concerned. Judge wisely and select with caution.

Ultimately a connection with an individual on any level – be it friend or partner – is really down to one's personal palette, but there are a few signifiers or warning signs we really cannot ignore. And for me, sitting right at the top of that pile is a man's desire to be adored more than he is prepared to adore back – a trait that's always going to be problematic to deal with. The amount of male Cinderella's out there attention seeking left, right and centre is just unbearable. It's all about you not him. In his eyes, you have to be more important, it's as simple as that. In every successful relationship I have ever witnessed, the man has always been the worshipper not the worshiped. Right from the start we are looking for a little twinkle in his eye that says he is determined to win over his potential Princess and for that to happen, he must adore you more than you adore him. A man that truly adores is unlikely to stray and in my opinion, that is the secret to achieving longevity in any relationship between a man and woman. Be the adored not the adorer – please remember that even if you take nothing else away from reading this book!

And the important bit to remember here is not to downgrade on any such expectations either. All those thoughts in your head of what Mr Right should and shouldn't be are important detail. We are talking about the rest of your life right now, so don't settle for anything less. Personally I have never been comfortable with the idea of settling in any aspect of my life. I think it's such a depressing state – especially if you are of the mindset that you only live once. Imagine looking back at your life and feeling wholly unsatisfied. It doesn't bear thinking about really. I know Rome wasn't built in a day and sadly no man is perfect, but what I am saying here is do not ditch all hope of finding Mr Right by hooking up with the first thing that comes along who seems to be semi-decent. He doesn't need to tick all the boxes, but he does need to tick a lot.

Many will disagree, but as I say, I don't think you should ever settle with a guy because you think he is nice and somebody you could grow very fond of, or could be good for you. It never really works in the long run. Eventually you will get restless and that's when the boredom of such monotony really sets in. Why do you think so many relationships fail in the long term? A lack of that all important *intrigue* I talk of – driving things forward – was generally missing right from the beginning that's why. How many couples do we all know that tend to split once the kids have flown the nest twenty years in, if not before – and the reason? There was nothing left to talk about. And that's because this 'click' we often refer too wasn't truly there in the first place, because if it was – in most cases – it usually lasts a lifetime.

I've had many conversations – I suspect like most of us – whereby people have told me that the love for their partner grew deeper and more fulfilling over time. Of course it does and will. This is the dream after all. But in every successful relationship I have witnessed, when the couple in question really stopped to think about it, at the heart of their first meet was a sense of intrigue and a little fascination about the person in front of them that fundamentally drove them on to date two. Settling in any sense of the word was never part of the equation. They wanted to find out more about each other instantly and that's the bit to hold on to here. If you're feeling that upon a first meet and in the days that follow, you may well be on to something. When the physical 'clicks' for you, that is the first barrier knocked down, then it's all about the intensity of an inner connection, which is obviously the really important bit and to be fair, can and probably will be a subtle grower until it really hits. Trust me, you'll soon know about it when it does! Falling in love is never forgettable. But as I say, the important ingredient in the first instance is that initial intrigue and fascination which basically underpins everything. Some might describe it as the chemistry between two people. And I am not just talking about the early days either, I think the very best relationships hold onto a piece of those first meet emotions for a lifetime and if I am ever asked that all important question in the future of what the secret ingredient is for finding a lifelong love – this paragraph will be my answer.

Right, let's talk some more about general qualities. A perfect Prince must firstly possess a masculine strength that suggests he has the courage to stand up and fight no matter what the cost to protect you. Be it in a professional or social setting, in this game, loyalty is everything. Gold dust some might say. He must be prepared to stand shoulder to shoulder. And you mustn't be afraid of putting him to the test in a social situation either. Let him put his money where his mouth is to prove his worth. You'll soon find out if he is all mouth and no trousers. Analysing his behavioural patterns in general to see just how loyal and genuine he really is during the early 'getting to know you' stage, also helps us separate the wheat from the chaff, without having to waste too much time. Keep an eye out for a wandering eye too. If he's checking out every pair of legs that walks past your table on date one, just imagine what he would get up to on the stag do. Judge how he interacts with other women right from the word go… nobody wants a dirty serial cheater on their hands.

Now we could spend much time talking about the finer detail i.e. he must be generous and affectionate, kind and polite to friends etc, but I am taking all these bog-standard qualities for granted. Yes there should be a fluidity and ease to your conversation. And yes his eye contact needs to be confident and unashamed. But a real gent will supersede these basics to hit super-hero status, thanks to that little extra something I call 'star quality'. A super fine specimen will radiate a certain charisma that is rarely seen in the common man. Trust me, when such a creature comes knocking at your door you'll know about it, for every part of your being will be shook to the core and this lady, is what we are on the hunt for!

A guy any girl would be proud and honoured to have on their arm and call their own. Mr Right will ooze originality and sizzle with spontaneity. A real Prince will go way above and beyond a cut-price margherita, or a 2 for 1 date night down the local. Yes, a keeper will be driven to thrill by presenting the unexpected. And that doesn't mean I expect him to whisk you off for a weekend of passion in Paris on a regular basis – although that would be welcome of course – this statement actually has nothing to do with personal wealth levels, or trying to impress with obvious romantic clichés. I am simply talking about a little extra effort on his part to bypass the obvious from time to time – a total must for long term happiness in my opinion. Basically your man needs to possess a desire to woo big time and it's your job to keep him hot on his toes in achieving this. Mr Right loves nothing more than a challenge, it's in his DNA.

Technically speaking, your perfect Prince will be driven to succeed like any other true Gladiator going into battle for the very first time and like any superhero-in-waiting, he needs to be tested on a daily basis. He should also be a master of observation, picking up on all your personal likes and dislikes, allowing him to focus on all the things in life that interest and excite you. The man may detest the idea of a night drowned out by the dulcet tones of an Andrew Lloyd Webber musical, but if it pleased you, he would and should grin and bear it. Suddenly such a sacrifice becomes even more attractive and seriously hard to find I know! Sadly most men have been spoilt way too much by their Mother's to be quite so flexible, but if he demonstrates a keen desire to wow and does not present himself as a closed book – just expecting you to fit in with his way of thinking – well, I think you may have just pulled a right bobby dazzler. Let's face it, nobody wants to spend their life in the shadow of a man, but unfortunately many men do just expect their partners to fit into their way of thinking. Not for you girl – lead from the front I say.

A protective beast that will shield you from evil, Mr Right will also have the power to openly express his inner emotions – again, a rarity in most men I know. But in this instance, the perfect Prince will be comfortable in sharing his personal thoughts and feelings with you because there is no doubt in his mind that he can trust you with his past, will be loyal to each other in the future and most importantly have a genuine desire to just make the other one happy for the rest of your lives. And no I am not talking about expressing himself through the theatrical medium of contemporary dance here ladies – that would be weird. Ideally nothing quite so Andrew Lloyd Webber, because if he enjoys that musical a little too much and turns on the theatrics – we may have bigger problems on our hands to deal with! More on that subject later, there will be no Lycra or tap shoe shuffle kicks at this juncture fingers crossed. My actual point here is the minute someone feels comfortable in revealing themselves, is the minute you know you can trust them and that comfortably leads into the loyalty thing. And yes, guess what – it does all start with a bit of intrigue and fascination with each other in the beginning… I am still harping on about that one!!

As in life, you need to think like a winner to become a winner and this is a vital quality every Prince must have to confront with vigour, all the challenges that a lifelong partnership can throw up. Strength not weakness thrives in the jungle ladies. And never dismiss the power of wisdom either for it is the greatest of aphrodisiacs. A wise man who offers an opinion on anything from Politics to the fickle world of Celebrity should not be dismissed lightly. No-one will ever get bored of a man who has something to say. And anything that ignites a passionate debate is always good in my book to get the pulse rates rising. Obviously if his vocals make your skin crawl, then Houston we have a major problem, but being genuinely interested in what a guy has to say, is a sure fire sign you have stumbled across a find.

Yes the man of your dreams must be riddled in reliability and always be on hand to pick up the pieces of a broken jigsaw. Breaking that down – the boy needs to be good in a crisis. And may I also remind you that chivalry is most certainly NOT dead in my World! A gallant set of good old fashioned manners is something to be treasured in the 21st Century. A gentlemen rushing to open your car door, or simply taking a moment to stand, and properly greet you on arrival, makes a girl feel fabulously feminine and a little giddy inside. It's almost non-existent nowadays to see a guy offering up a coat if a lady is cold, or an umbrella if the rain is pouring, so if it does happen, get out the bunting and celebrate. These are characteristics to behold and in real terms – a total turn-on! A Prince that makes you feel treasured is one to be thankful for ladies – this is a two-way street honey – it's not all take and no give. I guess when you do break it down, the idea of a man being strong and protective is much more appealing than the alternative – it's a primal thing – and essentially taps into four key qualities a keeper really must possess: depth, sensitivity and sincerity which ultimately leads us to the most important trait – honesty.

Yes the 'H' thing is of course a vital quality that sits neatly next too that all important other buzz word of the moment commonly known as 'trust'. There is so much to say when it comes to these particular subject matters and a topic I am sure many of you have debated for hours with the girls over a few glasses of vino on a warm summer's eve, still none the wiser on securing a fail proof formula for by-passing any potential heartbreakers and finding a man that can be trusted to keep it in his trousers. And don't worry, you are not the first or last to be fooled by certain playboy tactics either. Some guys are simply masters of disguise in such an arena and sadly none of us can truly predict or know what the future may hold with any individual, or indeed understand the behavioural patterns an individual may develop further down the line. We can however, be on our guard for the most important trait of all that gives us the best fighting chance to grab a Prince that ticks both boxes when it comes to honesty and trust. And what would that be I hear you ask?

Well, I purposely referenced this point at the top of this chapter because I think it's the most important and lies right at the heart of any successful opposite sex partnering. The lines can blur a little with a same sex union, but my personal observations tell me that a man who has the potential to adore a woman and is not desperate to be adored more, is always more likely to be forever faithful over any other. I cannot reiterate the importance of this point enough. Take a moment to reflect on the most successful relationships that surround your world and I bet I am right? It is quite simply the most important quality to be identified in any potential partner very early on and not necessarily something any of us would instantly think of. Yes, many of the characteristics I have spoken about here would be obvious choices on the tick list, but in my opinion, they all link back to this one point – the man must adore you more.

I am also pretty sure that as you have sat reading this chapter, most of you will probably think I am utterly barking and have totally lost the plot. A man possessing such qualities is either extinct or never existed in the first place right? And to be fair you are probably right, but the fact is, if you have the adore/adored ratio the right way round, if he's not already half way there in achieving this little lot naturally, he soon will be once you have moulded to your specific requirements. For a man who adores wholeheartedly can be anything you want him to be. He will be utterly blinded by your fabulousness. So actually – it turns out – the Mr Right you have been searching for your whole life really is out there! And you get to design him.

Of course there is one hugely important characteristic I have purposely missed out in this chapter that will be on the tip of everyone's tongue. Yes, being able to make you laugh and smile on a daily basis is the obvious choice we all reference when considering the ingredients for an ideal match, but I believe that drive to make you laugh and smile on a daily basis always starts and ends with this 'A' word I keep obsessing about. To put it bluntly, you and only you should be his obsession and number one priority. The one thing he cannot get out of his head like a stuck record. And if that kind of energy sparks – a totally organic connection that just evolves and cannot be faked – I believe you have probably found a man that will do no wrong by you and also deliver the happy ever after you are searching for right now. The 'A' is for Adored by the way, just in case you hadn't figured it out!

Vital Statistics

Right ladies, let's get to it, in the words of Madonna, 'strike a pose there's nothing to it' – yes, it's time to hit the visuals! Ditch the deep and meaningful for a moment and embrace our inner-superficial. Did I mention this read was going to be a bit of an emotional roller coaster ride? One minute thought provoking and the next damn right ridiculous. Mind you in saying that, the visuals are of course your first trigger to a potential flutter, so actually this is serious stuff. The physical connection is at the heart of any decent relationship and the warning signs for separating Prince from pauper are pretty easily identifiable to be fair and in some instances, you can simply ditch and run before a conversation has even begun. Here's my lowdown on a few vital material no no's, random rules you mustn't ignore and some friendly advice for when things get intimate. Ok let's randomly start with…

Cartoon character underwear
I did say this was going to be random! I am certainly not suggesting it would be appropriate to take a peek on first meet but, if and when things do progress in such a direction, please note that comedy pants on any level carry long term mental health implications and have the potential to scar for life. I mean what individual thinks it's ok to have Bart Simpson pop out and greet you whilst getting intimate? The last thing you need at such a juncture are the words 'Don't have a cow man!' screaming right back at you. Undergarments in general should be

classic, clean and of one colour. A touch of Klein or something similar will do very nicely thank you. A real Prince would not be seen dead in a pair of Bart's… and don't even get me started on comedy socks.

Hooped earrings
Yes sadly they do still exist and suggest this particular chap has not moved on since the eighties and unless you are prepared to invest in a complete image overhaul, it might be wise to do a Craig David there and then. As in – walk away – to find a guy that screams 21st Century.

The teeth
Now a rotten set of ivories are never going to be a massive turn on, but if he has the whole Brad Pitt a la Fight club gangster chipped tooth thing going on, well, nobody could blame you for getting a little over excited and in the mood for digging into a bit of rough, but in general, a lovely rack of pearly whites is what we are after. A man that takes pride in his oral hygiene and scrubs those bad boys good 'n' proper is obviously desirable. And if he flosses too, well there's no stopping either of you – this truly is the stuff dream teams are made of. His Mum taught him good.

The finer detail
Pay close attention to any rings, bracelets, watches, or indeed general trinkets – slash heirloom regalia – that may be visible to the naked eye. Wearing treasured belongings suggest a guy is happy to wear his heart on his sleeve, by paying the ultimate homage to those nearest and dearest to him. Such a move not only means he's seriously genuine and all-round proper nice by nature, it also demonstrates an affection for family life. And if you are thinking babies further down the line, you would be foolish to miss such an important signifier. If only such a fine specimen

could be bottled and genetically reproduced on a factory line – I would be a very rich man!

Whilst on the subject of accessories
Cheap Bad-Boy-Bling and garish-glitz styling might be fun for a night, but it's certainly not a ticket to forever. A Rolex on the other hand tells me you have totally hit the jackpot and like Cinderella herself, you shall indeed go to the ball – only this time it ain't over at midnight! Yes lady, destiny has dealt its cards and you shall live the life you were born to be accustomed too. Quite clearly, such an encounter must be fatalistic and on a purely superficial level, such accessories gives one an insight into the potential bank balance of an individual and let's face it, a true Prince needs a few zeros in the safe right?

Tattoos
Any sign of those L-O-V-E and H-A-T-E knuckles and I want you straight out that door girl. A singular fully tattooed arm however – or as they call it in the business *A Sleeve* – can be rather intriguing and will often allow you to unravel a potential suitor's subconscious inner thinking, whilst ultimately revealing a huge amount about their character in general too. Yes 'a sleeve' can by mighty sexy on the right person and although I know such body art would not classically be associated with a Prince par se, we are re-writing the history book here people and there is no such thing as set rules – which are clearly always meant to be broken anyhow. A rebellious streak can be a powerful aphrodisiac after all.

Grubby tips
Besides being utterly vile, dirty nails suggest an extreme lack of attention to detail and this is never going to be an alluring trait in any man. If he doesn't care for personal hygiene, he's hardly likely

to be bothered at making much of an effort with anything at all and that includes you. Unless he's a mechanic, I am not interested.

Hairy back – don't go back?
I know the thought makes most of us feel a little weak at the knees – and not in a good way – but in my opinion we can offer a little slack here people and simply point out that a quick tidy-up next time round would be preferable. This is not a deal breaker, more a re-training exercise in grooming maintenance. The same rule of course applies to the management of all bodily areas – both public and intimate!

Sandals and socks
Not even a hipster can rock this look.

Vest tops
Tight and with biceps bulging could mean we have a serious attention seeker on our hands and this is definitely not something we are looking for in the long term. Steer well clear. This one is a Fun-Time-Frankie and I doubt the word 'commitment' or 'monogamous' ever enters his vocabulary. In a similar vein, ill-fitted shorts that are a little tight in all the wrong places are another total no-no for me. Short shorts over the age of 25 are also unacceptable.

High waisted jeans
I am sorry but this look totally went out in the eighties. And don't even get me started on double-denim. Unless he is an authentic Cowboy fresh from the ranch, such a vibe is a total no go. Double denim means double trouble in every sense of the word. Again, a suitably fitting pair of classics is all that we require. When you think about it, one's denim is a fashion staple, so if the jeans are bad, I dread to think how the rest of his wardrobe is panning out.

Yes if he's a fashionista the slim fit, tight fit, extreme whatever fit might work, but no matter how cool he is, nobody can ever carry off the dreaded black belt, blue jeans and black shoes combo – this look is even worse than the double D combo. Something I never thought possible.

Tucked-in shirts
Again, always problematic when teamed with denim basics. Think geography teacher on a school field trip. Actually, on second thought's – don't!

Rubber soled shoes with an incredibly thick wedge
Great in a thunder storm, not so great in the visuals department.

Non-branded shoes and trainers
If he's not prepared to invest in a decent pair of runners, I doubt he is going to swoop in and woo you with anything more than the offerings of a fast food outlet either. And if the tight arse is openly proud about purchasing said foot ware from a discounted store – or worse a supermarket chain fashion department – I would terminate the interaction there and then.

Going for gold
Sadly too much of it can mean inadequacies in other departments. A true Prince would never need to rely on the value of a precious metal to impress.

Fake tan
Waking up with your white sheets lathered in the fake stuff is always going to make for an awkward conversation – especially if it isn't yours. A Prince should always tan in moderation if at all.

Breath
Minty fresh ideally.

Eyebrow shaping
Clearly no lady is ever going to dig a monobrow, so again, a little trim to tidy up this very visual of areas is more than ok. Extreme shaping on the other hand is just a little too much me thinks and should be left to the ladies of the house.

The scent… my vote goes to Tom Ford
Give me a bottle of his finest any day of the week. Hello boys! Bold and bombastic is my Eau De Toilette of choice. Yes, a sexy scent is most definitely the way to a girl's heart. What's your poison? And more importantly, does he have it? Who needs star-signs when we have Hugo, Gucci and Armani to guide us to our destiny!

Hair essentials
A guy desperately trying to hold on to a patchy head of hair when his follicles are quite clearly a little thin on the ground is often a sorry sight to see. Shave it all off man! Rock the bold, but beautiful look. Now you may or may not know this, but it's believed bold men are actually more virile than a man with a full head of hair. Ironically, although most men see boldness as a weakness, many ladies (possibly including yourself) actually recognise it as a rather attractive attribute and therefore we should always encourage any man to go forth and hunt out the razor where necessary. At the other end of the scale, the great thing about having to deal with an untamed head of hair is that you get to shape 'n' style to your own personal liking a little further down the line. So even if the locks are a little dodgy upon first meet – although not ideal – don't dismiss if you like the rest of what you see, just try and envisage his look when you have styled as desired… you will break him eventually. As a general rule however, long hair of any variety really should be

whipped off at the earliest opportunity – unless of course he is a sexy surfer, or you have a particular penchant for a hardcore head of the finest. A super severe side-parting also concerns me, as do extreme blonde highlights... homosexual tendencies springs to mind. Over familiarity with a pair of hair straighteners is also a warning sign regarding the latter. I am just saying. Genetically, its believed men follow the hair history of their Mother's Father, so if you want to take a glimpse into the future, this is the best place to start.

Body definition

Is obviously desirable, but nobody likes a show-off muscle Mary. A six-pack might be all well and good in the beginning, but when he's practically set up camp in the local gym you may regret such encouragement. Ultimately we want ones Prince to be obsessing over you not their body! Yes pert butt cheeks, a toned torso, bulging biceps and thighs you could crack walnuts with are all a lovely addition that's for sure, but being a gym widow should not be high on your agenda. In the same vein, an apron of belly fat wobbling about the bedroom isn't really ideal either is it – what we are looking for here is a bit of balance, or a happy medium some might say? A gent who is proud of his overall appearance, but not laying awake at night panicking about how to perfect his peck muscles. And anyway, a lovely little set of love handles never did anybody any harm in my opinion!

Overly-themed

There's literally nothing worse than a guy who's stuck in a fashion throwback time warp unable to let go of a bygone era or decade. Not only is this a tragic fashion statement, it also suggests we are dealing with a man who is clinging onto his past for dear life and that means one of two things: a) he's a desperate Peter Pan, or b) he's fully loaded with unresolved issues. Either way, it's a disaster and at this stage of the game are you prepared to burden yourself with such cans of worms? Statement t-shirts scribed with a profound quote or anything Hawaiian – unless fancy dress – is also a total no-no situ. I do own the latter FYI, so this is advised from personal experience. Such outfits worn on a day-to-day basis do not demonstrate a fun and creative edge to an individual they just tell you he's a total knob.

Overly-styled
A labels Queen also means one of two things: a) he's self obsessed, or b) he's gay. End of.

It's all in the jacket
If it looks a little skanky and in need of a damn good scrubbing the question kind of answers itself. And don't get me started on leather jackets. Yes, when timelessly styled correctly (think Beckham/James Dean) they do look super hot, but the Del-boy eighties look on any level is just ridiculous. What is my obsession with the eighties all about?! Anyway, the days of teaming with a polo neck and gold chain are long gone thank goodness, but my point is, if he's walking around in a moth ridden wreckage, just imagine what's going on underneath?

Suit ownership
Basically he must own one. We are talking staples here people. Has he never been to a wedding or worse a job interview? Hail that taxi and don't look back, I am welling up into a mass of hysteria just thinking about what misery the rest of your life may hold. Talk about lack of experience on every level. This is not the making of a Prince me thinks. If however, he loves nothing more than to rock a tux of a Saturday evening soiree, I am pretty confident you have hit the jackpot my love. Such events sound star-studded to me. 00Heaven springs to mind!

Celeb look-a-likey

Channelling an obvious A-list look is so totally #cringe. And a name dropper is even worse.

Eyeing up a bearded wonder

I don't care if it's on trend or not. Just say no to unkempt beards! I mean, who in their right mind is prepared to kiss a guy when half his masticated steak dinner still lingers in the undergrowth of his facial hair? It's just plain unhygienic. And unless you are Tom Selleck NOBODY – including Kevin Webster – can pull off a tache.

General advice regarding sportswear

Tracksuits in whatever form are highly offensive unless a) going to, or b) coming back from a sports related activity. And if he tells you he wears such garments for comfort, I should think very carefully before you make your next move. Grab those granddad slippers people – that's about as much excitement as you'll get out of a guy who wears tracky bottoms for comfort… at home or otherwise.

White sock hell

Teamed with trousers or shorts makes my skin crawl. Not meaning too sound overly dramatic – and I can freely admit I might be prone to a little over-exaggeration here and there – but please, this look is just hideous to the point of being mildly perverse.

Slip on shoes

Unless they are a brogue, or worn at home with a pair of classic Prince-like PJ's, I am simply not interested folks.

ATTENTION! Quick safety statement…

Be warned, too much polyester could be bad for your health. One misguided strike of a match and BOOM that bad boy is up in flames. Certain bodily movements including a vigorous walk verging upon a light jog, may also cause manmade fibres to ignite. Again, you may find such a statement dramatic, but there is always a price to pay when one downgrades on the fabrics we surround ourselves with. An allergic reaction might be the least of your worries. Polyfester (and no that was not a spelling mistake) is not on my menu… 100% of anything that isn't fake is what we are after here ladies. The same rule applies to your potential beau too!

Body parts

Without steering directly into the territory of the obvious, it turns out this is one area that very much ticks the personal preference box. I know. Who'd of thought it? An actual opinion that you are allowed to make at this juncture of the chapter feels ridiculous when being guided in such a specific – some might say – Draconian manner. When I let a friend read over this section of the book, she asked if I was on drugs?! Reach for the skies I say and keep those expectations where they should be. Mind you, in saying that, we really mustn't negotiate on a man whose eyes are just too close together. Untrustworthy apparently. It's an old wives tale that bases the theory on some sort of genetic mutation of untrustworthiness from years ago. Ridiculous I know, but I have never been able to forget it. Yes, for some it might be about a perfect pair of manly hands, others a nose so big it could sniff out a bag of chips drenched in salt and vinegar from half a mile away. The list of course goes on. Some individuals even find feet attractive? Simply unthinkable in my book! Whatever floats your boat I guess? And of course, more than a handful is just a waste right?! Oh, FYI and totally related. If you want to check out his sex face before delving down that road, get him to pump up a tyre on a push bike. Random I know, but all that thrusting is a total eye opener on the facial expression front.

In-situ visuals

AKA is he styling-out the occasion? Get ready to analyse ladies. How's he rocking his look, be it dressed-up, dressed-down, on the beach or pool-side (just say no to budgie-smugglers)? Fundamentally all we are asking/searching for at this stage is again, a little effort on his part. In fact scrap that. A LOT of effort on his part! Effort equals interested, which turns intrigue into adoration and that eventually ends in marriage.

Smoking…

Is no longer cool it turns out? And remember just say no to drugs kids.

Chinos

Wow, I cannot remember the amount of drunken debates me and my lot have had over said garment. It's ridiculous and I don't even know why? What are your thoughts? They really aren't that offensive are they? I feel the whole situation has escalated beyond my control regarding their appropriateness – or lack of as the case may be – between my friends and I, but oh what amusement it causes us. Personally I have always wanted to own a salmon pink pair. Perhaps writing this book will spur me on to make a purchase in homage. Will keep you posted on that one!

Listen I could go on and on with this chapter, it brings me such joy, but we have to wrap it up somewhere…

And yes it could be fair to say that in reality this chapter verges more towards the superficial rather than something of substance – like a serious debate on solving first world debt for example – but, ripping his look apart into micro-detail is a hugely revealing exercise of both taste and character. Not to mention being highly entertaining too. A tad picky some might argue, but last time I checked, pushing for perfection wasn't classified a crime? Yes a re-tweak here and there will probably be necessary. No man is truly perfect as we all know. But he does need to rock-out a bit of a swagger from the off, that makes him stand-out from the crowd and demonstrates he is relaxed yet confident in his own well thought out shoes… long as they are not budget of course!

The Dating Game

Breaking that all important third date barrier – to be in with a fighting chance of securing something of substance – can often prove to be a challenging affair. And in the same vein a little relentless too. I know they say you have to kiss a lot of frogs, but surely not a frigging coach load right? In reality girls, you need to summon every ounce of stamina you possess to persevere through the chaff to hit that wheat. It may seem daunting at first and once you're in the thick of it, a little gruelling at times. But like giving up smoking, it's all worth it in the end. Fingers crossed you might be lucky and hit the jackpot early on in the game. A good friend of mine pops out babies like she's passing wind, while the other can barely move – and that's only 6 months in. None of us know which way the cookie's gonna crumble in life. But one thing is for sure, you won't find out unless you try and both heart & head tell me that perseverance always pays off in the end.

Now in the beginning, the dating game is all about assessing your potential suitor. Sounds a little cold, verging upon dead inside I know – it's meant too. Decisions you make at this stage in the process will ultimately shape your future. Don't over analyse or over think it – this will only add unnecessary pressure to proceedings – just consider carefully whether 'the date' is ticking all the right boxes for you. Ultimately of course, when you find that real connection you're searching for, the small detail can be over-ridden, but – and it's a big but – if there is a doubt in the beginning never persevere. That doubt will grow, maybe not in the first few months, but year's later down the line when knee deep in nappy shit and with no way of escape. Don't be afraid to try and try again until something sticks – and I don't mean the nappy shit. Yes the dating game takes the stamina of an ox to survive, but your perfect Prince is out there somewhere and you will know when you've hooked a winner. The irony is, I bet you'll stumble upon a potential suitor right when you least expect it and these are the ones that often make the biggest impact. I have seen such situations end up in marriage.

There is no such thing as a time limit on finding true love either, so why panic and settle for something second rate? Love can hit at 19 or 90, simply go with the flow and enjoy your time in the moment right now (single or otherwise), because if you take a calm and measured approach, love often has a funny way of finding you anyhow. And in many respects, what other choice do you have? Desperation is certainly no aphrodisiac and not an option. Personally I prefer the other end of the spectrum, taking a what-ever kind of attitude to the whole thing. And bizarrely, by not taking the dating game too seriously, you instantly become hugely desirable whilst you're at it to the opposite sex too. Life really can be full of strange ironies at times!

Actually when you think about it, 'the dating game' is quite an odd expression really. It's not a game it's a quest. But as I say, the trick is to play the dating game at its own game and enjoy it for what it is – a bit of fun… taking such an attitude really will help lead you to something more fulfilling – especially if you don't constantly stress over it. And yes I know what you're thinking, when it comes to having children there are time restraints, but by re-booting your mindset in general and taking that 'what-ever' approach to it all, the desired results you are looking for will be delivered (pardon the pun). Ultimately of course it is a balancing act because the effort you need to put in to this quest should never be watered down, but at the same time, stressing out over it all won't deliver the desired results either. Commitment to the cause in a cool collected manner is what we are after.

And I know having Children is a hugely important part of many people's lives, but surely not with someone second rate? It's a mistake that so many people make, leading to years of unhappy marriage 'for the sake of the children'. Are you sure you would want to exist in such misery? I think not. If you are desperate for a child right now, why not turn to a gay best friend for assistance! At least you know you're likely to always get on and have the child's best interests at heart. No, when it comes to finding a man to spend the rest of your life with, a serious rumble in the jungle is what we are after and nothing less. A tingle deep within that says you are on to something – the L word ideally – because the exciting bit of course is when the dating game turns into a reality…

But before we move forward and whilst loosely on the subject matter of mindsets, lingering self-doubts can also do one from this point going forward too. We have spoken of this before I know, but now is the time to really get to grips with this subject matter if applicable to you. And be honest with yourself girl, I am not talking a few nerves here – I am referring to heavier anxieties holding you back. And if that fear is linked to a sense of rejection you can let that go of that one immediately too. You need to be open to the possibility that love is going to come knocking at your door and part of that is handling the rejection when it doesn't work out the way you want it too. The perfect fit is a two way street and that is what we are focusing on here, anything else is irrelevant. Don't waste time and energy mulling over something that isn't clicking.

As I always say, there are enough times in our lives to be upset or anxious about something outside of our control, so when you have the power to manage such emotions – seize it – and move on. Nobody ever looks back and thinks to themselves, 'well, I am glad I fretted over that for weeks and for no real reason or positive outcome'. My Mother also taught me something similar in that you won't hit 75 and think, 'oh thank goodness I stayed late to finish all those invoices 10 years ago'! You just reflect on the good times when all is said and done – a great philosophy I live my life by – because it's way too short to be worrying about the detail that's for sure. And men that bring nothing to your party for that matter!

Anyway in my experience, people don't tend to pick up on what (we) consider flaws, or moments when (we) fear the wrong thing might have been said. Well, at least not as much as we think, or feel they may hold on to as a judgement. Such irrational anxieties are generally a root cause of self-doubt in a social setting and pretty unnecessary they are too. In reality, these are simply are own insecurities talking to us and very destructive they can be. I bet you don't lie awake worrying about another person's so called imperfections/social faux pas – or what they might consider an imperfection/social faux pas in their head? Exactly, we are all in the same boat on that one and in reality nobody cares or is that bothered about any such detail. We create such headaches for ourselves through the blind panic of trying to impress and please. Take the weight of such worries off your shoulders because it is unnecessary luggage. And anyway, never soak up that pressure to be the people pleaser like I often have done so many times in the past. Step back and let the guy do all the work to impress in this instance – not vice versa. It's very easy to slip into such a role you know!

Ultimately all these points we are touching on here revert back to having a positive outlook in general from the inside out. A total necessity if love has a fighting chance of breaking in to your World. And if you are struggling on that front, focus on the little things in life to be thankful for. Take it back to the basics. The fact you have food on your plate to eat and access to fresh water is a blessing in itself. And that's before you even begin to think about bigger things such as friends, family, education and financial security for example. Focus on all the positives and ditch unnecessary negatives. At the end of the day, making the most of life and what it has to offer has never been down to judging ourselves or our physical looks for that matter. It's always about enjoying what we have to be thankful for and contributing to society in a positive manner – appreciating life and its possibilities. A positive you on the inside will better accept and appreciate the physical you on the outside anyway. Worrying about how we look is often a massive barrier in moving forward for so many and that frustrates me because it is such a waste of time and precious energy.

What is it they say? Mighty oaks grow from little acorns. The same philosophy applies to fixing and maintaining a healthy well-being. Think positive, be positive and eventually it sticks. I had a conversation recently on a night out with a lovely lady in her fifties who said she couldn't understand why she was getting so much male attention later in life? I asked her how she was feeling on the inside and her response was that she had never felt better – confident, content and happy in life. And why I hear you ask? Well, because she'd stopped caring about all her insecurities so much. The woman was literally fighting the guys off with a stick! Even the twenty year olds were desperate to bag a piece of this red hot cougar. Radiance most definitely shines from the inside out and you need to bottle up some of that juice before rolling fully into this process. I have many friends who are riddled with self-doubt. And guess what, they are all single.

Right, let's move on now to the actual dating bit. Remembering that a guy likes to show a girl what he is all about – the dating game is his chance to wine, dine and impress. Or as some might say, an opportunity for him to show his true colours – your job is to spot whether they are indeed bright and shining. A 'Prince in Progress' is obviously the preferable option, who can be tweaked and tailored as desired! Date number one for example will either be: a) bizarre, b) perfectly pleasant, or c) shows signs of potential. Whatever the result, you will have a story to share with friends which can only ever be a good thing. Personally, I rather enjoy a first date once the initial nerves are settled and in-check. I am nosey by nature, so always interested in hearing other people's business – whether I fancy them or not. Even strangers! Just always make sure you are armed with some conversation starters and references to their profile if linked via online dating. Build on conversations already had and remember, a little nervousness on either side is a good thing, because it shows you care and have a desire to impress.

On the subject of a first date, keep it casual and avoid dining at all costs. The first dinner together should be intimate and reserved for a later date. Plus, if you do need a get out of jail card due to a total cringe on the conversational front, you are screwed if he orders three courses. Oh and as a general rule, don't sleep with him on the first date either. Or as a dear friend so delicately puts it, 'don't give it away like a bag of chips on the first night'. And that's not because I think there is anything wrong with such a move. I have never understood all this chat on waiting for the right time etc. When is the right time? Clearly when it feels right in my book! I just think you should make a guy work for it. After all, they do love the chase and thrive on a little tease. In fact, I believe it's considered an aphrodisiac!

Ok, from this point on we need to start thinking that you've bagged a potential and the dates are starting to flow along nicely. After all, this book is about visualising your entire journey from A-Z not just A-P. As I always say, positivity breeds positivity. It is going to happen and we need to consider the strategy for a happy ever after throughout your ride to the aisle of 'I do' – not just the initial meet. And on that note, you also need to get a sense of what a guy is thinking early on in the dating game in terms of where they hope the dates are going. I refer to this period as the 'phase of exploration'. The getting to know you bit basically. A time to find out whether you are both singing from the same song sheet so to speak. Obviously don't scare the shit out of him with talk of marriage and kids on date three, but do gage whether you have a potential keeper on your hands. And here's the thing, even if you do really like him, if he doesn't tick the majority of your desired boxes, you need to ditch and move on. I know it sounds horrific, but this is the reality of the game at this stage. It can be vicious and mentally exhausting at times, but you need to know if you have something serious on your hands or not and whether he's worth the effort. Establish that early on – especially if you have some pretty exacting requirements – having children being at the top of the pile.

Now, as time goes by with a potential that does click and you fly past dates four, five and six, I am hoping seven, eight and nine will continue to surprise and delight. Variety is the spice of life and as such, a potential keeper will whip up a mix of varied wonders that go way beyond the norm – he should be desperate to impress! The cinema, meal & pub combo is all well and dandy, but if this dating lark slowly turns into a pint down the pub every time, you know you're in trouble. Remember, this is the rest of your life we are talking about and *dull* is not on the menu. A true Prince will mash up the classics and throw in some spontaneous fun for good measure… with a Capital F! This is the kind of guy we are on the hunt for.

Don't be afraid to step outside of your comfort zone to try new things either – and by that I don't mean sexually by the way! Actually that is a good spanner to throw into the works because you had best establish if he's a bit niche on that front while you're at it. I mean, if you don't mind doing it with a cross dresser that is all well and good, but nobody likes a nasty surprise popping up in the bedroom – all jokes aside. And let's face it, such a fetish is generally a total game changer for most people. You may laugh, but strange things happen and it's often with the ones who look the most normal – whatever that means! The stories I could tell you and vice versa I bet…

Ideally Mr Right should make the effort to take inspiration from your interests and conversation pointers, whilst also throwing in a few surprises of his own. Expect nothing less. We are on the hunt for a Prince here after all, but if all else fails, a little nudge in the right direction never did anyone any harm. If you spark up a chat about always fancying a day trip to see the glorious sights of Bath – I expect him to book it on a whim. If you mention that it's been a dream and lifelong ambition of yours to take a hot air balloon ride, guess what – I want him to make it happen. At the same time, I expect him to take your breath away with the unexpected. Variety really is the spice of life folks and a real gent will get it right with some organised fun that doesn't feel forced. There is nothing worse in my opinion and yes, it really is all a balancing act very few men can ever dream of possessing, but it's always good to set a standard for him to aspire too. And remember, being un-cool is the new cool, so if he's a little off-centre every now and then, don't judge, go with it and dip your toe into something new, fresh and exciting. A moment of randomness is liberating. Never retreat into Mr 'n' Mrs Average who consider a Friday night with a curry and a couple of cans thrown in as a big night outside the norm. Live life on the edge not your sofa.

Going back to the dating timeline, when it feels right and a potential Prince has been bagged, the weeks will quickly turn into months before you know it. In my head I can feel the 'L' word blossoming and all being well you are going to fall pretty heavily girl. Perhaps month three could be a good time to encourage a weekend away. Notice I purposely use the word 'encourage'. That is not your cue to start organising anything. Drop hints and put pointers in his back pocket by all means, but don't take charge. Every man I have ever met loves a challenge, so go forth and set them girl. I think it all dates back to early childhood when boys are generally taught by their Father's that winning is always the end game. No matter how big or small the task is – every guy on this planet wants to hit the top spot and deliver the goods as it were. The dating game is definitely no different and I am often amazed that women do not tend to max this weakness in men to their own advantage more than they do. I say weakness because it is an outlet for a little control slash manipulation on your part that maybe you didn't even know existed?

It always surprises me in general actually how much women tend to take the weight of the World onto their shoulders within a relationship. Why not pass over the headaches and let him solve a problem once in a while? Men are quite lazy by nature and will step back if you let them and that's when a relationship can start to flat-line and fizzle. Continually push your man to exceed all your expectations and he will be constantly driven by that desire to leave you speechless. Ok, so I will cut a little bit of slack at say 6 months in. Throw the boy a surprise treat as a gesture of good will for doing so well. A bit like throwing the dog a bone – I can guarantee he will bounce back for more! This is a strategy for life not just dating FYI.

Moving from dates into 'dating' is a pretty organic process of course once all the relevant foundations are in place. Obviously this is where the adventures really begin, especially when both parties are sensing that they want the same things out of life – even if an official conversation hasn't happened at this stage. Just always remember that a real Prince will be guided and take the lead (in every sense of the word) from your pace not his.

Let's Talk About the Gift-List

Now I am throwing this chapter in here, firstly for another spot of light entertainment and secondly because the best bit about the dating game is that it should get you some – gifts that is. Ignoring the totally obvious, let's take a closer look at the very good, very bad and very ugly possibilities from the World of dating regalia… they often say much more about a bloke than you could ever possibly imagine. Here are my all important findings -

Top 10 turn-offs

Anything Cubic Zirconia

Faking it – especially diamonds – is never going to cut it. A girl wants to shine bright like a real one right? Yes it may seem like a minor detail at first (easy to dismiss), but trust me, this is just the beginning to a life full of fakery. Lies, deceit and treachery springs to mind.

2 for 1

It just doesn't sound sexy does it – a BOGOF (buy-one-get-one-free) – dinner date. Yum, book me in! And don't get me started on 2 meals for a tenner. Gross! And if you find him beaming with pride from ear to ear over a mere £5 saving for whatever the reason, I predict a *plain Jane no nonsense* existence for you my girl. The fact he's even using some sort of discount voucher whilst on a date is horrific! To clarify – 'Budget' and 'Date' are not two words that should ever be associated or mixed together. Being as tight as a ducks arse is definitely one trait that isn't fixable in my World.

A Cuddly toy

Cringe not cute. A totally noble gesture for pre-pubescent teenagers, but from a grown man, it's just a little bit wet, desperate and pathetic. No offense, but we are on the hunt for a turbo charged beast here ladies not Mickey the flaming mouse.

A collection of cheesy love songs

I swear I just dry wretched writing this. It really doesn't get any worse than a home-made collection of all the classics. Traditionally a CD of the very best would be delivered and became quite a trend back in the 90's, but just because he's bang up to date and zips over a download list for you to check out, doesn't detract from the facts. In the very fine words of Kate Moss, 'it's basic bitch'!

A single red rose

How very eighties. Hello, catch up with the 21st century people. There is a World of delicious floral fantasies out there to explore and delight with, so why settle for the obvious? A dodgy bunch of buds from the local petrol station just doesn't cut the mustard with me either. I suspect I am preaching to the already converted here. Get those runners on girlfriend such a guy needs to get some experience under his belt before he's ready to sweep you off your feet.

A framed photograph

Of anything is bad enough, but if it's of himself – OH M G! The words *huge* and *ego* spring to mind. And if he rocks up on a second date with a snap of you both, just imagine all the other creepy cuttings pinned to the attic walls – psychopath stalker alert!

A personalised poem or song

Dress it up any which was you like, a public recital of any kind – especially that of a poetic nature – is always going to make you wish the ground really could sink beneath you. In a private setting and a few dates further down the line is possibly bearable if it's his thing, but in a public space is just unthinkable – especially when only a few dates in and sober!

Anything diet or fitness related

Again you can beat about the bush as much as you like with this one, but in a word, he's basically saying you're fat. A fitness DVD for Christmas, a year's gym membership for your birthday, or a recipe book of low-fat healthy shake ideas for breakfast, are all total no no's. Walk girl.

Cheap classics

I am of course referring to our Nation's favourite three: chocolate, undergarments and perfume. All of which are totally fine and dandy as obvious staples in the World of dating – my problem in this title is the *cheap* bit. If he's going to do chocolate it should be bespoke, if your Prince is delivering a fragrance it should be well thought out and if we are talking naughty underwear, well, his selection should be expensive. Mr Right should be showering you in luxury – period. If he can go out and chuck £100 away on a night out with the lads, he can certainly afford to purchase a decent box of choccies for you to enjoy every now and then.

Personal essentials

Any man who thinks a pair of pyjamas and matching slippers is ok as a dating gift on any level needs to be ditched immediately. Such a talent is barely worth saving from himself let alone having intimate contact with anyone else – especially you. Talk about unsexy. In the same vein, a boring bottle of bubble bath will always be a boring bottle of unoriginal bubble bath – unless of course he asks to jump in too! And if he even dares to go anywhere near personal hygiene (especially oral) – or worse – intimate grooming products (we can all sniff out that hair removal cream from a mile off), I would most certainly evacuate via the nearest exit.

Top 10 turn-on's
Now this is what I am talking about ladies...

Anything precious metal
The clue is quite clearly in the title here. It's precious my love! Just like you. Huge hugs and heavy petting all round. And if it's antique or heirloom, get the bunting out girl. I feel a wedding coming on! A well thought out piece of jewellery suggests this perfect suitor is in the mood for longevity.

A puppy... or a pussy
I was trying to resist the 'everyone loves a pussy line' – purely for self-entertainment purposes – apologies, an obvious gag I know... just couldn't help myself. Of course in reality, we all love a fury friend and yes it's all a bit Paris Hilton, but really, how could you say no to a perfect lump of loveliness jumping straight into your arms on date five? Ok maybe that's a bit full on, but further down the line would be a masterstroke move on his part in the art of wooing big time. Granted it might be a tad spontaneous and a bit of a challenge on the practicality front – but hey, who cares! Clearly he's planning on spending the rest of his life with you by making such a gesture.

A hardcore handbag
And when I say hardcore I mean hardcore. Step away from the shelves boyfriend and head straight over to the luxury counter.

Fickle as a fish I hear you cry again? Ab-so-bloody-lutely! A sophisticated scent wrapped and waiting for you inside said bag would always be a welcome addition too. This is how you present the staples people. In-fact, anything on the top-end beauty front will do – besides anti-wrinkle of course!

Something for your home
Superseding expectations would most certainly include a commissioned piece of art for example, or a bespoke item of furniture, but in the main, I will settle for anything that has personality, style and a little bit of thought behind it. Some say that a super-posh scented candle is a little par se and obvious nowadays, but for me, such a gesture is a total winner – especially if he links-in to your favourite flavours. This is the kind of attention to detail I am talking about ladies. Obviously anything tedious – I am primarily talking kitchenware gadgets here – are clearly warning signs not to be ignored. Does the man want you chained to the kitchen sink for the rest of your life? What are the implications of such a gift? Vases and pointless ornaments in general, that you just want to chuck out the window should also be deemed inappropriate and rendered useless.

A pair of Heels
I feel a Cinderella moment coming on! And guess what? It's sponsored by Louboutin too. Yes you SO totally will go to the ball with this kind of a keeper. And if he's clever enough to team with a seductive selection of sexy underwear – well, put it this way, I big time bagsy front row at the wedding ceremony.

A ring!
What was that I was saying about diamonds earlier… engagement or not, you've hit the jackpot at this stage of the game my lovely.

A romantic getaway – five star style

It's a classic and you just cannot beat it. A weekend retreat just the two of you? Yes please, this is a man that means business. And guess what, he gets my vote hands down! But remember, the drama is always in the detail. Yes, booking a weekend away is a great move on his part, but to add that all important extra x-factor, he needs to wow you with what goes in to the itinerary… and not just in the bedroom department.

A hardback book

Intelligent, sexy and thought provoking are the words that spring to mind immediately. For me personally, this is the ultimate in romantic gestures. The title selected, its content and the story behind his literary choice are of course key. But if he gets all those essential ingredients right, he is on to a winner and so are you.

A Charitable donation

A clever move on his part to woo and woo some more. If you take the time to share a personal tragedy or story close to your heart and he's inspired to act upon it by supporting the cause, we can only but salute the man's efforts. This is the work of a true Gent who is determined to impress beyond the superficial by demonstrating a depth most men can only dream of. This turn-on ticks a lot of boxes for me.

A single cupcake

Is the new red rose. Beautifully boxed, delicately detailed and again, drizzled in your favourite flavour is a total winner. Sounds a little sickly I know, but don't knock it till he's bought ya one. It's a seriously sexy move, especially when sharing – it would be rude not too!

Parlour Games

Time to ditch the eye to eye contact ladies, let's talk getting physical. Yes the act of getting intimate is utterly integral to making any partnership work – clearly I don't need to tell anyone that! The icing on the cake that literally binds two people together is exciting stuff and at the heart of any perfect matching of soul mates. The question is, what, when and where should it all kick off? Will that first embrace get the heart-rate soaring? Should there be a dramatic build-up to the act in question? Or should it all begin and end with a bout of heavy petting in the first instance and no more? When is the right time to cross over the line... so many questions and so much to think about?

Personally I don't think you can beat a good snog as a pre-curser. Yes, a little re-training is sometimes required to hit the desired spot, but in general, that first snog sets the tone for what happens next and how marvellous further investigations may well prove to be. And quite often that's all it takes to whip those fruity pheromones up into an uncontrollable frenzy. Physical attraction is one thing, but that first interaction can take things to a whole new level of fun. If all you want to do is rip his clothes off there and then, things are looking hopeful and the future may indeed be bright. Ultimately, the physical connection between two people and its impact on head, heart and soul is what elevates any relationship into the 'L' word territory. Remember, we are looking for a lover and partner here, not a new best friend!

And in answer to my question about having so many questions and so much to think about. Well actually, in short, there really shouldn't be any questions, or anything to think about for that matter either. When it comes to sex, just let nature take its course. Don't delve down the road of unnecessarily mentally exhausting yourself over the rights and wrongs of your actions for no rational rhyme or reason. In reality there is no right or wrong when it comes to this subject matter in my book. Such rules – if you choose to listen – have been wielded into Western Culture & society and for what? The most ridiculous of the bunch are often the ones that haven't been questioned or challenged either. I am going off-piste a little here, because I guess this point applies to much of our daily lives. Many codes of conduct exist that all deserve to be ditched – especially those regarding a physical engagement.

There is no need to over-analyse or panic about what is the correct protocol for such interactions – it's all a total waste of precious energy. Simply letting rip on the physical side of things when it feels right for you seems like the logical answer to me. I doubt very much, debating such decisions will be first and foremost on your deathbed when looking back at your life! Go with your heart on this one. And anyway, over-thinking thing's is one of our biggest downfalls as human beings, acting as a barrier and wall to moving our lives forward that many of us don't even realise is there. Why can't I find anybody? What am I doing wrong? Are questions I get asked all the time and when I tell people that maybe they are holding themselves back inadvertently through their own actions, it can often prove to be a bit of a light bulb moment.

It's a challenge to break such a cycle for sure when stuck in a certain headspace, especially when you want something so bad, but it doesn't seem to be happening. And I know this from personal experience, but the minute you allow a moment of rational clarity or thought to sink in, is often when the answers or solutions you have been hunting for naturally form around you. By forcing yourself not to over-think or question your actions – especially the small ones – everything that is the 'right' thing to do just seems to slot into place. This rule of thumb is so relevant across every aspect of our lives – especially when forming relationships.

Anyway, back to sex! To clarify, I am not promoting a quickie behind the kebab shop on date three here – although whatever floats your boat in the moment I guess – I am simply saying that you shouldn't bog yourself down with the details of it all, religious beliefs aside. If the chemistry is electric why delay the inevitable? Don't let such a moment get lost in transit. Acting on impulse is thrilling – even more so when it comes to this particular subject matter. And whilst you're at it, ditch any pre-conceptions about having to hold off because he will think you're 'easy' in any way. That is not how men think. They rarely think like that if they REALLY like a lady. The idea that the longer you make a guy wait for any physical activity, the more he will want you is totally ridiculous. If anything delaying such an engagement will just make him frustrated and we all know how that can end up – limp! We could indeed go round in circles for days questioning and debating what a guy may or may not think about you sleeping with him on the second date for example, but as I say the truth is, he will probably think absolutely nothing of it whatsoever. If a guy is head over heels for you, thoughts on your sexual conduct will not even enter his consciousness. Don't get cut up about him judging you in any sense because I guarantee he won't be… annoying how we never have these sorts of conversations about a man's conduct hey? It can still be a very one-sided world sometimes, even in the 21st Century.

In reality women question everything, whilst men question nothing. But as we all know, men certainly don't think with their brains and thus the good news here ladies is that the power and how it manoeuvres lies very much in your hands. As I say, we could debate this subject matter for hours, but in my experience, both protocol and society's moral compass goes out the window anyway – by both parties – when 'that' connection is made and why? Well, because it is so rare to find, we all want to embrace and hold onto it – or in this case get on it for the first time! Only one thing on the mind as they say and when us humans are in the midst of falling into the L word (I am talking lust here), we find it very difficult to think about anything or anyone else for quite some time – particularly when moving from lust into in-love.

Talking of pressure (or it's build-up as the case may be),the notion of having to aim for this one big magical moment of intimacy after a few dates also has the potential to put a proper damp squib on proceedings moving forward – especially if it needs a little work in the beginning. Rome wasn't built in a day darling. And anyway, I am all about the crescendos in life me. Hitting pitch perfect from the off leaves us with nothing to aim for right? Or maybe I am just trying to convince myself of this theory for my own well-being! Clearly a session of spectacular love-making is unbeatable be it date one or not and never tires however many times you repeat it. But I guess in reality – for many of us – the first time generally involves going out on the town, getting a little intoxicated to take the edge off any pre-show nerves and waking up the next morn having done the deed. Obviously not too shit faced. Nobody wants a drunk chucking up over their shoulder during such moments of intimacy, but by opting for such a strategy, you get to step back in the saddle the morning after the night before to perfect your work – practice makes perfect after all. Surely that cannot be a bad move to kick start proceedings when all is said and done?

Now in terms of parlour protocol, I always recommend letting him take the lead initially. This is a chance for your potential Mr Right to really prove his worth. Remember we are looking for a Prince here ladies not a Pauper in the bedroom department. An under par performance is not on the agenda. Most men like to showcase their skills in the beginning as an assertion of their masculinity, so don't deny him off that opportunity. A girl needs to feel sexually desired and adored after all. Further down the line you can freestyle all you like. If anything, don't be afraid to experiment once you have found your feet with each other. Having said that and as I mentioned before, it's also important to establish any niche desires on their part early on in the dating game because let's face it, dogging and domination really isn't everyone's cup of tea! But I guess some would say don't knock it until you've tried it, so who am I to argue. Joking aside, at the other end of the spectrum, even a Prince amongst Men can have the odd malfunction here and there, so if at first you don't succeed try and try again – especially if you think he's worth it.

A natural chemistry can sometimes take a little time to ignite, so be patient and let a potential Prince find his feet so to speak. Ideally it will be a click 'n' go situ, but that's not always the case. Sometimes you need to learn how to fit together, but quite often that kind of union can be the best fit long term – especially if when it clicks it really clicks. But whenever those magic sparks do decide to start flying – be it date one or five dates down the line – the early days are ultimately a chance to explore and discover each other's likes and dislikes in the bedroom department. And don't be afraid to let go and throw caution to the wind on this one. Let your hair down girl, it's time to party! Surprise him, excite him, thrill him, but most importantly keep him on his toes. Mix it up lady. Even play the vixen every now and then! A real Prince always likes to break a routine. All you have to remember is that he must never ever be allowed to take you for granted. Make sure he's subtlety reminded of that every day. If anything, it will make him desire you more.

WARNING! When Mr Right Turns into Mr Wrong

In his eyes you're probably swimming along quite nicely a few months in, but if for any reason it doesn't feel right, don't be afraid to quit the game early. Better to reboot at that junction rather than two years down the line when things could get messy. And sadly it is a desperate sinking feeling all too many of us can relate too. Clinging on for dear life in the actual hope we may be able to fix a potential long-term relationship, when in reality, there is no chance of recovery – not without professional intervention anyhow – and that is certainly not something we should be considering for survival at this stage in proceedings. The amount of conversations I've had with friends discussing the pros and cons of 'giving it a try' is exhausting. Deep down we all know if it's never going to work so why bother delaying the inevitable? How can we ever fix something that wasn't ever right in the first place? Recognise red alert situations ladies and be brave enough to act swiftly and accordingly. I know I sound a little dead inside, but in the search for true love, one often needs to take a cold hearted approach if you really want to bag the very best and not waste precious time. A mistake often made by too many if you ask me.

Trust those precious instincts of yours for they are rarely wrong – especially when it comes to men. Women have a sixth sense for such things so don't ignore them. If he kicks off all guns blazing and you sense a bit of *Tom Foolery* going on to simply tempt you into his lair/boudoir at the earliest possible opportunity, you are probably right. He is only after one thing! Dinner at his for a first date is always a good sign of such an intention. And if that's all you are after then fine, but don't be blinded into thinking you can change him eventually, because 9 times out of 10 you can't. If ultimately he's just after a one night stand, he's generally just after a one night stand and nothing more. On the other hand, if he seems a little too good to be true – and yes I know this is clearly a hypocritical statement based on the content of this book – once again, you are probably right. When it feels like someone is putting on a show and not really showing their true colours, they generally aren't. If he's displaying behavioural patterns that you don't trust, never choose to ignore such gut instincts because it will be a move you live to regret. As we all know, the fundamentals of trust and loyalty are absolute vitals in general for a relationship to succeed… and of course a few laughs along the way too!

All this talk of one-nighters leads me nicely onto my next point. Sadly most guys (under 70) do think first with the apparatus they have been gifted with, but if it's all that drives him, well, he will be a creature very difficult to contain. Have you ever tried taming an animal of the wild? No, me neither, so why bother with such a feral beast in the first place. And again, I am not saying be a frigid bore here, I am simply highlighting a few warning signals of singular intent on his part and of course characteristics you should look out for. And although you might think these are obvious points I am making, when you really like somebody it is very easy to avoid facing them, putting off the inevitable until impossible to ignore. I guess it's really just about keeping an eye out for the devil's who only think about the outcome of an evening when on a date – not you as a person. Walk with caution when it comes to motives and tactics.

Always ask yourself – is this really how I imagined my Mr Right to behave? This is generally where your answers lie in their most basic form and in reality should always inform your actions. What would Britney do? Is my go-to place when difficult questions need to be raised in my head! If nothing more it makes me chuckle and laughter is often the best medicine for clarity. Yes sometimes in life we all need to make decisions that are hard to reach and may cause problems for us in the short term, but deep down we know it's the right move in the long run. Never shy away from any such situations that could be easy at first to ignore. Face these challenges head on, otherwise you will look back only with regrets not happy memories. It's a mistake made all too often by us humans in this journey we refer to as life. And when it comes to relationships, it's not only a vital clog in hunting out *the one* – it's also the secret to enjoying a happy existence too. This task of sifting through the dregs was never going to be easy girl, but when one is on the lookout for perfection, one has to de-sensitise to it all a little. Sadly we all know utter perfection doesn't exist – ourselves excluded – we just need to watch out for the following walk-away situ's that would be dangerous to ignore…

Up first for me, are those wandering eyes – the ultimate sign you have probably ended up with a wrong-un. Wandering eyes equals a wandering mind, and a real Mr Right will always be focused on trying to excite, impress and surprise only you, instead of spending his time trying to identify a new target to pursue. On the same lines, if his texts, emails and telephone calls slow down, so has his interest in you. Ditch and run. Don't waste time mulling over a thousand possibilities – this is when the new dead-inside you comes into play. Time to move on to bigger and better things!

A date cancellation or late arrival is also a total no no. As is his desire to wrap up a date early. He should be gagging to see you. Why would a man obsessed ever want to wrap up a date early? You should decide when a date begins and ends – not the other way round. Get proceedings in order girl. And if he feeds you some cock and bull about having to be up early in the morning, well, the warning signs are clear for all to see. Oh and if the classic 'I have to work late' excuses start flowing in, be unforgiving too. Unless it's a really extreme reason, working late regularly just doesn't cut it for me. If he really wanted too, he would find a way of getting out of such commitments, because let's face it, all rationale goes out the window when we feel like we've found *the one* – getting up for work in the morning is the last thing on anyone's mind. The 'Practical Pam' in all of us is put on the backburner for a while, whilst the powerhouse of passion aka *the honeymoon period* freestyles a little.

Of course, at the other end of the scale, we must also address the needy ones who are beyond enthusiastic, texting and calling every five minutes, declaring their undying love and utter devotion. Talk about a total turn off! There is a difference between adoration and a wet lettuce. This is a guy who will literally be happy with anyone. He is obviously beyond desperate to be loved by – yes you've got it – anyone! Such a soul has issues only a professional can unravel and that is not for you dear. A full on freak that is psyched and enthused to a point that he needs to be medicated to maintain any level of normality is obviously not an ideal candidate for lifelong happiness. I am talking extremes again I know, but I wasn't born a drama Queen for nothing.

'Middle of the road' is another expression that really bothers me. Why would anybody want to be middle of anything? It's so uninspiring. I have made it my life's work to be anything but. Although I do believe it comes rather naturally to me! Indeed, all potential Princes-to-be need a bit of edge without the attitude, whilst at the same time being comfortable and entertaining on the social interaction front with friends and family – all other applicants need not apply. Balance on all levels is the name of the game and judging how he is with those nearest and dearest to you is never a bad thing to do in terms of analysing his true character. Ultimately it's a case of ditching the needy desperado's of this world, to focus on the finer forms of the male species. To clarify, outlined below are the key stock types to watch out for:

Fun time Frankie's: Focused primarily on a doner and quick bonk at the end of an intoxicated eve. Not an ounce of depth in site.

Mr Re-bound: Beware of the, 'I've just come out of a long term relationship' conversation. The interim date post break-up only ever ends in disaster. We all need a little time out post anything serious let alone a lover.

The screw up: Can we fix him? No we can't! We can only ever mend ourselves not each other. If Mummy didn't love him (which is generally how this story starts), he needs to address that heartache first before committing to anybody else. Don't attempt it yourself. Step out of the situ and leave it to a pro. There is much to be said for offloading anonymously and for that matter, not revealing way too much about yourself to a potential partner too. The past does have a tendency to catch up with us all at some point if not dealt with and resolved in some form. However, the end is not totally nigh with a screw up – who by the way are often very easy to fall for – if they are really serious about healing and moving forward on all levels for both themselves and for the sake of a relationship. My overriding problem here is that the screw up's often morph into a bit of a socio/psychopath in the end which is never going to be easy to live with or ignore.

The insecure flower: Needs a good kick up the arse, but has a chance of being saved when he realises you are for keeps and he starts to believe you truly have the hots for him. This one requires perseverance, but there could indeed be a light at the end of the tunnel if you are happy to work for it. Ultimately, making him man-up will be your full time job for a while girl! And dealing with weak willed minds can be an exhausting business – are you ready or even willing to fight this often excruciating challenge?

Following your head in the beginning and letting your heart run wild when you know you're on to a good-un is a great philosophy to live by I find. Ok for a quick flutter of fun who cares, but if we are thinking long term, it's always head first people. And whilst on the subject of mental health: manipulation, intimidation, or psychological control on any level must not be tolerated from any man. Even if he is drop dead gorgeous, which again the sociopath variety generally are. When a guy makes you feel inadequate to meet his exacting standards it's most definitely time to walk away. I cannot bear boys who play mind games. A real crazy will hold back for a while, but will usually kick off with a little tease (generally over weight or looks) that can escalate and manifest out of control. No man should ever joke about such sensitive shit. These initial signals of 'banter' always lead to full on misery further down the line.

In the same vein, no-one should ever be made to feel anxious to please, or reliant in any way on another individual – these are all classic signs of complex insecurities on their part. Recognise and acknowledge any such behaviour and be brave enough to move on… quickly. A man who is intent on gaining such control over you is not worth knowing. Talking of insecurities, the feeders are the worst. The guys that encourage excessive eating and drinking are a dangerous breed to watch out for. They may seem completely normal, but there are hidden depths to such characters. And I am not talking about a few excess pounds most people gain when content in a new relationship. I am talking serious food intake here facilitated by them. Clearly a man who behaves in such a manner has some pretty serious issues to deal with, but that isn't and shouldn't be your problem.

And yes, we are dealing with some extremes here and yes, most blokes actually are decent, but it's my job to cover all the bases and most of the time that means dealing with the darker side of the species. In fact, finding true love is more about warning signs to watch out for and walk away from, rather than what you should be trying to find as such. What you can't buy, or find, or put into words, is what we are all looking for I guess and kind of sums up what being in-love is all about. Nobody has a formula for that one, but being aware of what you really shouldn't be on the lookout for, or clinging on to, is probably half the battle won. At the same time, don't be afraid to ditch your classic type and test-drive a few new models to see what fits, you might be pleasantly surprised by what you find – I've heard such tales end in marriage!

BEWARE! A Few Signs that Say Your New Beau Might be Gay

For some, it is a near obsession. What if he is gay? How can I tell if he is gay? Have I turned him gay? Has he always been gay? The conversation is just gay gay gay. Of course I have no magic wand or Jeremy Kyle type lie detector test to assess said sexuality, but I can take this random opportunity to point out some tale-tale signs that might steer us in the right direction…

Sorry, it's a top thirteen as I could not cut down to a classic ten!

Madonna or Kylie…
Is not a question any straight boy should be asking!

He said what?
Listen all guys like a good gossip, but boys tend to just overview or touch the surface, whereas you and the girls can spend an entire evening ripping a subject matter to pieces, whilst whipping up a million possible answers. If he falls into the latter camp and digs a little too deep for comfort, there may – as the song goes – be trouble ahead. Only this time there will be no moonlight, music, love or romance.

Shelves or Counter?
To be honest, he really shouldn't care either way. A gent obsessed with the latest advances in anti-ageing worries me. I am talking

beauty products here ladies, and if he owns more than you, herein lies a big problem. Now don't get me wrong, I am fully on board with the luxury indulgencies a branded beauty counter can offer. Who could ever question your desire for a classic potter to sniff out the latest wonder treatments? Certainly not me, but if he is swooping the floor like an uncaged animal on a desperate hunt for skin perfection, I guess we can safely say there is cause for concern regarding said sexuality. And if he suggests a date that involves a mani or pedi, I think that cause for concern would not be unfounded.

Hey girlfriend!

Straight boys are NEVER friends with straight girls without either one fancying the other -FACT. I always come back to the same answer when in debate on this very contentious subject matter as previously discussed. Listen, if he is piled high with a gaggle of 'platonic' girlfriends and always knee deep in conversation with them, either he is extremely popular with the ladies and a big fat attention seeking womaniser – which obviously raises some important questions regarding his potential level's of commitment to you in general anyhow – or underneath it all, he's secretly gay and gagging to gossip on all the latest celebrity happenings in Heat Magazine or via Daily Mail online. Either route is clearly not ideal.

Busy hands

I know it's a total cliché and I am being very stock about all this, but gays do have busy hands – especially those who often prove to be overly expressive in all areas of their life… I feel a contemporary dance coming on!

I get so emotional baby…
Of course it's good for a guy to show a bit of an emotional side, but blubbing over Long Lost Family, Surprise Surprise, or an X-Factor Power Ballad just leaves me feeling cold. Put it this way, if you get into a fight over who's next in the queue for a table at Nandos, you want to know your man is gonna be prepared to fight for that spicy hot chicken pitta right? Reflect ladies reflect.

The cubic-zirconia test
Now this one is very simple. If he identifies cubic-zirconia as fake diamonds without hesitation and he isn't a jeweller by trade, well, the odds are seriously stacked against a positive outcome in your favour when it comes to his sexuality I am afraid.

Boys don't B-I-T-C-H
Well subtlety they do, but not as much as girls 'n' gays – and in my experience never as vicious!

Let's get physical
Or not as the case may be. If he harps on about saving himself for the wedding night, or there is no evidence of a previous partner in a physical sense, I would firstly panic and then seek professional intervention to assess the situation. Religious beliefs or performance related issues are my only get-out clauses here, because most guys are keen to fast track to this bit of a relationship at the earliest opp and happy to repeat said process as much as is permitted for that matter too. Anything less should be questioned.

Showtime
5, 6, 7, 8! If he adores nothing more than a night of show tunes soaking up the very best of Andrew Lloyd Webber's (clearly I am addicted to him) latest extravaganza on the West End – or worse a local Am-Dram society production of Annie for example – I

would most definitely reflect on the actual potential of your future happiness together.

I don't do DIY

Why not would be my instant response? If he's all soft furnishing's & interiors and not interested in the fixtures & fittings it's time to start questioning his orientation. Every man should have a decent tool box right?

Boys or girls

Who's he got his eye on? We are subconsciously drawn to admire the human form we are naturally attracted too. Spontaneous reactions cannot be tampered with or fought against. He might be riddled in denial, but you can't fight nature people – however hard an individual might try.

Mad about Her Majesty

A Queen loves a Queen after all.

Of course, a quick flick through his internet history on any chosen electrical device will help quash any rumours and internal niggles I am sure. Not that I condone snooping, but if you find anything to do with dark rooms and lube, well, it turns out you probably won't need to have that awkward conversation after all. Not ideal I know, but on the plus side, I guess at least you'll have clarity on the matter? But hey listen, this chapter is primarily for entertainment purposes only, fingers crossed this little lot need not apply and you can fast-track right through the dating game and into the 'partner' zone post haste. And on that very note – it's time for us to get serious!

Part 3

Marrying Mr Right

The Big Investigation – Family, Friends and Everything In-Between

Oh sir, just one more thing...

It's in those finely tuned words by the late, yet very great Lt Columbo, I take inspiration for this next chapter and realise, there is no such thing as too much information when it comes to finding Mr Right. As a relationship moves forward – and in true Jessica Fletcher fashion for that matter too – it's important to delve a little deeper to make sure it really is a potential match made in long-term heaven. The proof may well lie in the pudding, but how can one be expected to perfect a recipe without the right ingredients? I want to know exactly what's going on in his kitchen cupboards both physically and metaphorically and so should you.

Of course when you hit this stage of the game, it's more about supporting and resolving together rather than taking the ditch and run approach. Clearly things are starting to turn into something pretty exciting – especially when considering everything we have already spoken about and potentially overcome to reach such a point. And that's an important thought to keep hold of. Sadly I doubt many people take the time to assess how things are going or even consider such a conscious investigation, but in my opinion, that is where so many go wrong. Assessment is everything in the quest for long term love and ultimately, a key point we seem to come back to again and again in this book. So why stop at the final hurdle?

And yes many will argue against this fact, reverting to the classic 'what's meant to be will be' type statement and nature will take its course etc, but I believe this to be only part of the equation we should rely on when trying to find longevity in a relationship, the results and reality of which, generally only come to fruition ten years down the line – which I guess is half the problem. Now don't get me wrong, I am usually a go with the flow type person myself, but in retrospect, this has been my own downfall in some aspects of my life and probably why the divorce rate is so high in this country! Going with the flow is not an ideal philosophy for life. Being decisive and guiding one's destiny really is which is exactly why such an investigation into your potential Mr Right is so important.

Perhaps I didn't even realise it myself until I started writing and considering this subject matter so deeply. On a subconscious level we are constantly observing a partner, but the point is we need to make it more of a conscious thing, to better inform our decision making processes before we commit for life. In some ways, be a little more academic about it all. Rational caution is never a bad thing anyhow. And that doesn't mean don't take risks, it means you must take calculated risks in life, which in turn will always make the consequences seem easier to live with. I am very much a live for today not tomorrow kind of guy, but have learnt through experience and my own mistakes that a little focused evaluation along the way can prove to be a rather helpful tool to utilise in all areas of our lives. Of course we can also be overly cautious and too analytical which can stifle progress, so yes it is all about balance, but when we recognise that balance and get it right, taking the time to consider our next move is generally a useful one.

Right lady, now is the time to rip his world apart and delve right in! Yes everyone has ghosts in their closet just make sure he isn't hiding an entire troop of them. If you sense he's holding something back, now is the time to unearth. And tripping up those nearest and dearest to him is often a good way of finding out. Drunken mates down the local always prove a useful source for intelligence too. And remember, you're overall strategy is to simply be interested not inquisitive. Nobody likes a prying eye on the hunt for detail, but if there is any heavy stuff from his past you need to know about and deal with – friends & family are usually the one's to spill first.

Ok yes, you could wait for him to reveal all at his own pace, but hey, why not just fast track so you can put to bed and move on. A problem shared is a problem solved after all. As I say, we are dealing with some worst case scenarios here girls. Fingers crossed there won't be any such baggage, but if there is, it needs to be dealt with swiftly, and anyway consciously acknowledging each other's weaknesses in the first place will only ever make your relationship stronger in the long run. Understanding the person you are falling in love with is something people often forget to make time for when wrapped up in the whirlwind of it all, but in doing so will actually help mediate any bumps along the road that may arise in the future. Recognising why someone reacts in a certain way to a situation and what triggers that reaction is half the battle in resolving it.

Don't get me wrong, some things are obviously well worth holding back. He doesn't need to know the exact number of notches on your bedpost for example. No man wants to hear that. They like the idea of being the special one anyway, so why deprive him of such an accolade if he is so desperate to have it bestowed upon him? Nothing is to be gained from such a reveal. Airing frivolous adventures from ones youth is something I would save for a drunken conversation and in moderation to be censored where appropriate. Your potential Prince doesn't need to know everything about you, but you most certainly need to know everything about him – especially if keen to tweak and shape a little to your liking. Now is the time to start digging and I don't mean sexual conquests, just the detail that maketh the man!

For many people however, there is a fear of delving too deep as it could evolve into a state of jealousy over past relationships, but knowledge is power as they say and by uncovering everything, there are no surprises left to knock you off your kilter. Oddly more empowering than restricting, it will also help you get a real understanding of what shaped the person you are starting to fall in love with – some perspective in many ways. And don't be afraid to touch on his first loves, girlfriends, loss of virginity – the works. No holds barred as they say! And of course the fun times too – childhood, teenage years and university life. Being armed with a little roster of your own anecdotes and funny stories is never a bad idea too. It's actually rather liberating to reveal such details and in turn makes you realise that although our personal history impacts on both the present and future, it's really in the moment we live.

Now in terms of actual analysis, start with his family and work outwards. Do they appear sane and stable? Is always the first question to ask, or is there cause for concern? Does he have any friends? If not, why not? Is he happy in his chosen career path or striving to do better? Both are plus points, but if he doesn't really care either way, there is again a cause for concern. And on that note, how are the finances? A Prince should never be a pauper – full stop. I joke a little here, but being financially secure is an important factor for most. Much can also be said about a man and his castle too. An untidy house equals an untidy mind. A true gent will keep both in proper order and by the way, when I said rip open his cupboard doors I meant it! What's going on in the bathroom may I ask? As I say, being beauty product heavy could suggest we have a vanity Queen on our hands and no girl should have to deal with a man that spends longer in the bathroom than she does. Check out the contents of his medical cabinets too. If there's more to hand than your average local A&E department goes through on a sat night, we also have a full-on hypochondriac to deal with, which in my experience can be exhausting. And don't even get me started on the bedroom. If he's a total freak all will be revealed under said bed. I have found some strange apparatus in my time and needless to say, none of them particularly pleasant.

By nature boys can be dirty creatures of habit and highly inexperienced when it comes to day to day life skills too, but a real gent should know his stuff. If Mummy has been running around after him his entire life, you can bet your bottom dollar he will expect the same of you. Cinderella pre-ball is not what I have in mind for you my darling. And you may joke and consider all this just trivial detail, but trust me girl, it's like living with someone who has a differing taste in televisual programming, what starts off as a minor disagreement of opinion can escalate with disastrous consequences. Ok we all have to compromise – but by how far when it comes to your quest for lifelong happiness? The fundamentals of preparing a basic dinner, changing the duvet cover and ironing a shirt are all things we can teach, but is he prepared to learn?

A life – as in social, is also non-negotiable in my book. A full bodied bloke with a rich and diverse mix of hobbies, interests and friends suggest life is worth living and that is the kind of guy I want you to bag. A man should never be solely reliant on you for fun and a friendship group to tap into for that matter. Every day should have purpose for him, a sense of adventure and a little dash of spontaneity thrown into it. And don't be afraid to watch how he interacts with others to uncover how genuine he really is either. I am not suggesting he needs to be life and soul of the party, but when he speaks do people listen? A girl will never bore of a man who always has something to say and brings a decent conversation to the table. It's also important that he's prepared to step outside of his own social comfort zone and be by your side to step into yours from time to time – especially when needed for special occasions – anything less could lead to a very controlled and/or isolated existence.

And of course we need to consider his long term ambitions. You can't take a horse to water my love, if kids and marriage are your bag but not his – forget it. As I've already mentioned but must state again, convincing a man to get on board with your way of thinking on something so huge is an uphill struggle – there needs to be unity on that one. In the same vein, if he's all over the idea of you popping out a squad for the local five-a-side Sunday football league and you ain't interested, how on earth is the relationship going to pan out long term? It isn't, is the answer and such logistics are important conversations to have before ploughing on through to the sign off as it were. Ultimately you need to ask yourself if he is really ready to settle and if he has enough life experience behind him to fulfil yours. To be crass, if he's only ever slept with one person for example, will he be having affairs and a mid-life crisis at forty? Listen, there are no right or wrong answers here by the way, it's just a case of making a judgement call and sticking with it. Re-training exercises on the basics of life are not a problem, but the bigger picture is always a trickier ball to handle.

Adjustment and Transition

To reiterate from the previous chapter, I know it all feels a little cringe, but 'the talk' (as in about your lives going forward), really is a vital component and part of the final phase in securing you're happy ever after. It doesn't have to be a big drama, but it needs to happen if only to confirm you are both singing from the same song sheet as it were. Both thinking along the same lines in terms of marriage, kids, and how you see life panning out. Sadly as I say, this can be a sticking point for some and delving in blind, reliant just on the way you feel for each other can have dire consequences further down the line.

Technically though, the odds are seriously in your favour at this juncture and the only journey I see you planning is to the aisle of 'I do'! Surely any man that can make it through all the hurdles I have thrown up thus far is way above and beyond Mr Right material? It's a tough gig to hit the dizzy heights of the 'adjustment & transition' period and for that a potential Prince must be commended. But what does it all mean when we say adjustment & transition? I know it might sound a little academic, but in reality it's simply manoeuvring from your old life into the new one. A bit like the caterpillar transforming into a butterfly, it might feel a little odd at first, but in the long run it promises to be a thing of beauty. The soul mate has landed people! This is it! From here on in your mindset will have shifted from long term dating to super serious... and from where I am standing, the future looks positively dazzling for you. Remember positivity breeds positivity – the notion that none of this is going to happen is officially dead to you.

It's an exciting journey ahead from this point forward that's for sure. Sharing each day together and having that companion you have always dreamt of by your side is a wonderful thing. Like I need to tell you that?! Yes it can be a bit of a juggling act at first. Making time for friends (the true ones who support you no matter what) and family for example can be a challenge, but it is important to make the effort not only for your own well-being, but for a bit of balance in your relationship too. Don't suffocate yourselves by living in an insular world where only the two of you exist, because it's not healthy in the long run and eventually you will struggle to breathe. In the same vein, staying true to yourselves is also a vital clog in the longevity of a partnership. Don't morph into something that isn't you. Being in a relationship is not about always aiming to please the other person either, more about patience, tolerance and getting used to each other's little habits and annoyances, which can often be an endearing force that tends to grow and grow anyhow.

This leads neatly into my next point, moving things forward to a fixed abode. Your place, his place, or a neutral territory – such technical detail doesn't really matter – the important bit here is the official coming together as one and what that signifies. For it's in this moment you will truly realise you're not single anymore. And as I say, that doesn't mean you have to transform into a proper pair of 'Howard and Hilda's' existing in an isolated World of matching jumpers and fleece jackets, more an official statement/declaration of the leap you're making together. And I know sometimes a girl can panic about moving in on his turf even if invited to do so – well don't. If he wants you, he'll happily let you rock his Palace and smash his territory to pieces for that matter.

And anyway, I guess for most of us, it's standard to make such a move before marriage nowadays and religious beliefs aside, a vital step in my opinion. Not only to adjust and balance you're old life with the new one, but a chance to find your feet and really discover how the 'new' other half ticks. Getting used to the fact there is someone else to consider when making decisions and finding common ground when and where compromise is needed. Ultimately I guess, it's about taking the time to build foundations and allowing a workable structure to evolve for day to day life together.

Yes it's exciting times ahead girl, and although a little scary at first, the big move is a joy to behold and indeed a moment to treasure in sealing the deal as it were. And yes, I know technically it hasn't happened yet, but that honestly doesn't matter. Pre-empting and pre-planning for anything in life is one of the strongest positive moves we can take in helping make it happen in reality. This last part of the book is all about shifting that mindset of yours into one of anticipation and excitement not despair and desperation! Ok, I am being a bit extreme there but you get my drift. A little day-dreaming never did anyone any harm in fact I think it's good for both heart and soul. You should try it I highly recommend, because when you start to believe something will happen and map it out in your head it generally does. That is exactly why we are delving right into your happy ever after here too. Now is the time to bring the fairytale to life. Imagine it, get inside it and don't be afraid to immerse yourself in it. This is not the time for logic, ditch logic and embrace your imagination. Tap back into what a Prince Charming meant to you from childhood and bring the dream alive in the here and now, because if nothing else, such positivity is only ever going to make you even more attractive to the opposite sex than you are already and that – fairytale or not – can only ever be a good thing in reality. Screw all negativity I just cannot bear it and what does it ever bring to the party anyway?

Now as we all know girls, sometimes even a Prince needs a nudge in the right direction. So if when you reach this stage of the process you sense a little caution about the big move – not on it like a car bonnet, as some of my more refined South London friends might say – there are two potential outcomes. Firstly he's holding back for an actual vocal go-ahead from your good self, or secondly, he's just not that interested. Let's focus on the former right now because, if being honest, we all know the difference between a man stalling due to the fact he's not keen to commit and the man who simply needs prodding in the right direction. Taking appropriate action and not procrastinating on either scenario is the important thing. If he's ready you will know about it and a few simple hints will trigger the desired reaction. Spending 3-4 nights a week together is a good start, or even suggesting an extended holiday are often all the signifiers a guy needs to take the next step. It tells him you are in for the long haul and that is all he really wants to know.

Men work off instruction and sometimes they need to be guided in the right direction. Believe it or not, most guys are actually pretty sensitive creatures underneath it all and even the toughest need reassurance. Being rebuffed is very difficult for any man to process and many will often hold back until they know it is safe to let their guard down – more so than women. True, others will go gung ho straight in for a piece of the action, but personally I think the cautious souls are a safer bet in the long run. Not quite so irrational and off the cuff in their decision making processes. Some might argue that these kind of guys are less likely to cheat over a more calculated creature, but hey, that opens up a whole new can of worms that we could debate for hours! So anyway as I say, it's all about the initial instruction on your part – be it subtle or direct – and is a skill worth perfecting when keen to get your own way with a bit of subconscious manipulation. And when you need to, be very precise in your communications that certain rules broken will not be tolerated either and the consequences of such actions. Adultery usually proves a good place to start! But ultimately all jokes aside, from here on in it really comes down to one question... do you want to spend the rest of your life with this person? Remember this question for when the time is right because if you reply instantly and without hesitation – you have your answer.

Operation Aisle

I am slipping into a celebratory number as we speak – bagsy I bag the bouquet! I feel a finale coming on. This next bit of the jigsaw is all cakes, flowers and dresses – my favourite subject. And yes I am purposely going all x-factor on you because when you make it to this point in the story, having ditched said boil in the bag for one and only a Bridget Jones DVD for company, surely a moment of self-congratulation is permitted? And make it you will. On your terms and when you are ready to be whisked off your feet… pretty much any day soon then my love!

Clearly you have bagged a keeper if he ticks all the boxes to reach the status of marriage material and the only task left going forward may be to drop a very BIG hint that you are indeed ready to say 'I do'. Again a little nudge in the right direction is sometimes needed. Get him up the aisle girl and wielded to you for life! Any man that passes even half of my rigorous requirements is a Prince amongst men in my eyes. I have ripped the poor buggers to pieces and for good reason, so you can separate the good from the bad and at worse the ugly.

Now I am taking for granted that you will have physically sampled the goods as it were by this point – surprises on that front when it comes to the wedding night are not ideal. Try before you buy as the saying goes ladies! And although for many, marriage really is the icing on the cake, it certainly isn't for everybody and that's ok, but I guess primarily you just need to know he would be keen if you really wanted too. That's often all a girl needs to hear.

I guess marriage signifies the ultimate commitment and most people desire that sense of security. And beyond any financial benefits, in today's modern world where religion is not necessarily on the main agenda for so many, surely this is what marriage really stands for? Anyway, that one is your call...

Once the deal for forever has been sealed to your liking, this is where the fun really begins. We have spoken about it before, but now you literally have him in the palm of your hands for what my circle of friends describe as the re-training exercise. A light re-moulding of your man to meet your exacting requirements! They say old habits die hard, well not on my watch. Screw nature, it's all down to nurture when it comes to a friendly re-tune. And don't be scared, as I say, a mild dose of 'man-manipulation' never harmed anyone in my book – especially men. I only need to observe my own Mother at work to know that! It may be subtle changes, such as a mild overhaul regarding his fashion accessory choices, or a re-style for the follically challenged, but like any decent act passed in parliament – these particular changes are pushed through for the well-being of all involved. And too right I say. Whatever the issue, be it big or small, if it's a bugbear – redress it ladies. Trust me, THIS is the real route to lifelong happiness when all is said and done.

Talking of bad habits, the amount of men who do not wash their hands post pee is really quite shocking. Establishing acceptable hygiene practices is obviously paramount. Urine riddled hands caressing your body is certainly not ideal. I have witnessed more than I dare count leave a public convenience without washing said hands. It's outrageous and not necessarily contained to just a 'number one' situ either if you get my drift. The biting of finger nails may well be the least of your worries! Personally I recommend covering such basics at the earliest given opportunity.

Life Logistics also play a vital role when setting up shop together as briefly touched on earlier. It is a bit like living in a shared-house; you need to have the same outlooks to live harmoniously. If you are frivolous on the heating and electricity front, but the rest of the household is military when it comes to such subject matters you are in for trouble. The same logic applies to *life logistics.* If he eventually wants to live in Australia and you don't, once again we have a big problem. True love can be ripped to pieces over logistics. I have seen it happen many times and hence why I keep re-visiting it in one form or another. Resentment is an ugly force and can sometimes over-power the L word when not dealt with thoughtfully. Of course, everything in life can usually be negotiated and a common ground found, especially if the L word is strong enough – love can build a bridge as they say – just don't end up half way down the aisle with all these questions unanswered in the back of your mind. Talking is good people and that includes about the future.

Now this leads very nicely onto my next point – *The Proposal.* And yes we do need to start thinking about it even though it hasn't even happened yet! You read my points in the last chapter right? Let's bring the fairytale alive people. This show-stopping moment of a moment (when it happens) should indeed be a total show-stopper. Orchestrated perfection, that has been well researched, planned and executed. I want to see a slick operation that demonstrates a deep thought process on his part. A true Prince will grab such a magical moment by the horns and make sure it is a sensational scene to treasure forever. A living testimony of his undying unfaltering love for you – a quick pop of the question over a vindaloo really will not do. The real drama is always in the detail and I want drama with a capital D. Remember these words girl and get ready to judge when the time is right.

And anyway, once he's popped (for fun let's just imagine he has right now), you have a chance to really reflect and analyse his efforts. The last hurdle to impress some might say. His 'down on one knee' moment doesn't have to cost a fortune, but it absolutely must make your heart skip a beat. You know, sometimes the smallest of gestures can be the biggest, so I am really not being a size Queen here, just pointing out that said proposal needs to be utterly spectacular and a scene riddled with romance. At the same time, make it crystal clear and drop into a general conversation that such extreme efforts should never be considered just a once in a lifetime episode either. Striving to impress you should be considered his life's work. Now you see why I am pre-empting a little right? Nothing beats a little forward planning.

Why should you settle for anything less? He needs to understand that he hasn't totally hit the jackpot and probably never will. Tease with a 9.5 out of 10, or even a 9.9 out of 10, but never let him reach the dizzy heights of perfection. Nothing in life is ever perfect. Never let a guy sit back and think he has hit that jackpot, it will just make him lazy. Critiquing his gestures is a lifelong commitment I am afraid and keeping him on his toes is another.

Going back to the actual proposal for a moment, I was pretty gobsmacked to discover that the majority of women start subconsciously planning their actual wedding the minute they say 'yes' and that even includes Valentine's Night – not necessarily the most romantic of gestures. Screw the red roses and box of choccies, all you want to do is reach for the wedding planner apparently! But is this true do we think? Some of my friends concur and well, according to hazy research, an overwhelming majority of brides-in-waiting have a ready built picture of their wedding day in their head's even before the big question has ever been asked. In some ways, it all goes back to making that fairytale from childhood a reality I guess, but in my experience, most ladies are generally ready to say 'yes' way before a guy gets round to actually asking anyhow. I suppose this slight time-lapse allows for a bit of mental preparation and probably why the bride-to-be traditionally leads the charge on the wedding planning front? Basically you've had time on your hands to think about it! I bet the moment a man pops the question you'll slip instantly into planning mode and find it very difficult to think about anything else after reading this! Actually, I tested this theory out over a glass or two of vino with some of my girlfriends and they all came back positive. I guess when it happens it's hard to think about anything else and why should you.

Now obviously we don't need to go into depth on the wedding itself – I have another book for such detail – but it is important to reference what happens post proposal, because this is another exciting bonding process for you both to embrace and something you should have in the back of your mind – even now! A challenge that will bring you together like never before some might argue. Planning a wedding is a bit like learning to drive, get everything in the right order and all will turn out fine. Preparation is key, but here's the thing, whatever happens, don't ever allow yourself to morph into a bridezilla. A bride-to-be stressing out over canapés or floral table-centres is such a turn off for any man to observe and have to endure. I have seen relationships sour over such transformations. All your guests and husband-to-be want is a bloody good knees-up, so although the detail might be important to you, never lose perspective of the bigger picture.

This is it lady, the final frontier is in sight. The altar of L-O-V-E is literally within touching distance. Reach for that frock when you get here, head held high and ready to style it out on the aisle of *I d*o because you deserve it. And the minute you reach the last chapter of this book is the moment to embark on your adventure. I am not going to lie. An effort it will be my love, but my goodness the prize will be well worth it in the end.

Finally, not wishing to sound like a money-grabbing bitch, but if he stacks it way before you do, we need to know you're gonna get your hands on his stash thanks to that ring being firmly on your finger. Turns our marriage is actually a total must on second thoughts. You are a Princess after all and cannot be expected to work the nightshift down Asda's stacking the veggie counter. Self preservation is paramount. And who say's romance is dead? Not on my watch.

Happily Ever After

What a priceless recipe that would be, a definitive a-z guide to lifelong happiness… guaranteed or your money back. I can just imagine how the advertising banners would unfold – Love long and Prosper! Dreams really do come true in such a fairytale World. We all wish right? Well, maybe just hold that thought for a moment, because you could argue that it's our ability to feel any emotion in the first place that allows us to fall in love. And let's face it, the unearthing of a true soul mate is both life changing and a miracle of nature. A whirlwind of utter euphoria, reminding us why living life in any sort of neutral, is both boring and terrifying at the same time. Sometimes of course the extremes of our feelings can be a little much, but always remember, without the lows you cannot appreciate the highs, with the former making you greatly appreciate the other. And it's this sense of appreciation that sits at the heart of every happy ever after. Yes you will both have to work at transitioning comfortably into what fits in terms of day to day life, but never take for granted what you have found when you find it. Appreciate each other and always make time for each other.

Many have theorised over this subject matter and the debates could rage for hours. Yes part of me does always come back to the viewpoint of what will be, will be, but isn't that just being lazy when it comes to our general well-being? I am a fatalist in many senses, but I am also a firm believer that certain decisions do aid and guide our destiny. That is one of the great advantages of growing older – knowledge really is power. The more experience we get, the more informed our decisions in life become. Safer we could argue, but informed at the same time. Apply the same philosophy to your future relationship. Don't just get wed and think that the rest will take care of itself and no further effort is required. A 'ticking along' existence leads to an unhappy existence. Grab life by both hands, get out there and live it… together. This is the ultimate route to happiness not just for yourself but as a team.

Never stop learning about and understanding each other either. That journey doesn't end with 'I do'. There is a natural tendency to pull back a little on the effort front, which to be fair is only natural. You've bagged the Prince so why bother type attitude? Wrong. Don't ever fall in to that trap. Effort on all fronts is the secret ingredient to keeping the spark alive – even 40 years in! My very own parents are testament to that. Of course my Mother would put it down to having the patience of a saint, but its way more than just that to last that kind of distance. Dad doing what he is told always helps, but right at the centre of it all, is a deep respect for each other that never seems to fade. I guess this must all be down to what we cannot control – true love.

There is a lot of talk about the transitional struggles during the first year of marriage and how the adjustment period can take a bit of getting used to. Yes this it all true, but keeping the fun times rolling will certainly help take the edge off said process. And that means you too! Surprise, excite and be spontaneous. The same applies to this so called 7 year itch people speak of. Not putting any thrust into all areas of your relationship – and I do mean all areas of your relationship – is where potential problems start to manifest. Drifting or just existing can lead to boredom, which in turn can push either party to look outside the marital unit for fun and frolics. Recognise if there is an issue brewing between you as time goes by and act on it immediately. Talk to each other, don't ever let things fester or manifest into something bigger –

yes I am primarily talking affair's here people. Together you must ensure you keep life well and truly spiced on all fronts, because prevention is the key to preservation. Attention seek with each other not an outsider.

As I say, we are talking extremes here and some situations are obviously outside of our control, but if we all stop and think about our own experiences, even the watered down versions have some relevance. That job from hell is a perfect example of slowly falling into a depressive state – especially when it proves difficult to escape. Recognise a red light situ in life and do something about it before it's too late. Just say no to negativity and refuse to let any darkness settle for long. And if it does start to take hold in any form, both within the relationship and life in general for that matter – take action to rectify immediately. Routines breed boredom, whilst laziness leads to loneliness eventually. Don't end up as the couple who sit down ten years from now questioning why they are unhappy in a sexless marriage. When you start wondering where it all went wrong it's often too late to rectify. The five stone weight gain piled on whilst ignoring the rut of an existence and misery you have allowed yourselves to evolve within may hold part of the answer, but as I say, by that point it's a relationship beyond salvage.

Right let's move on now to talk day to day stuff. And with the potential introduction of tiny feet, a certain sense of routine has to be established, but even then please please break it up every so often because life should never become a boring 24 hours of structure, not just for your sanity, but for the sake of your marriage too, otherwise before you know it, you will be looking back wondering where all that time went. No-one likes a fun vacuum at the end of the day. And if Children are not on your menu, there really is no excuse! A little randomness is good for both heart and soul, as is a bloody good laugh. It's a bit like those spontaneous nights out that turn into a hardcore adventure. You really cannot beat that feeling next day – especially if you take the hangover out of the equation!

Post wedding, it's also important to keep your independent World moving forward. As I mentioned earlier, continue to enjoy quality time with friends & family, both alone and with your partner. In many ways I think the former helps keep him on his toes. A little reminder that you could easily survive without him! Probably isn't true by this point, but hey, he doesn't need to know that. Encourage independence, but make it clear where the boundaries lie. Going out for drinks with the lads is all fine and dandy, but a lap dance down the local gentlemen's club is probably not going to be acceptable for you. And of course, the best bit about separation is the coming together again.

Next up we need to talk duties and before all the equality banners are erected again, by that I don't mean dutiful housewife – I am addressing your duty to seduce, keeping his eyes wide open and heart melting. Men are massive attention seekers, so it's important to massage that ego every now and then, which in turn will keep him striving to impress you. The basic characteristics of our feline friends and the male species are not so dissimilar you know. Both are guided by instruction, discipline and reward in equal measure. Men are secretly dogs in disguise! The comparisons are ridiculously on point. Give him an inch and he will take a mile… with tail wagging – I could go on all day with this one.

Now remember, men really do love to be heard and whilst most women try to look interested in what they have to say, quite often there is a tendency to dismiss, or at worst ignore a profound statement and move the conversation on, particularly when being entertained by a gay best friend! Easily done I know. But straight men find this very frustrating and not in a good way. Listen and engage in a conversation he initiates – even more so in a group setting. Trust me, they love it. Give him a voice and look interested even if you're not. A win by his favourite football team is a prime example and whilst changing the tyres on the car may be dull as dishwater, a quick note of praise and recognition for all his hard work is all he is looking for. What happens when the dog fetches the ball? Exactly! And on the plus side, he will adore you back tenfold.

And on that note, don't forget the art of conversation either. I know that sounds stupid, but take the time and make an effort to really talk in a more fulfilling way than just planning out your next load of laundry. In many cases, talking is why people fall in love in the first place. And I don't mean you have to have a deep and meaningful on a day to day basis. Simply chewing the fat with your lover on your thoughts or experiences of the day will only ever serve to make a bond stronger than it is already. Intrigue might be considered the ultimate aphrodisiac in the first instance, but when you know you can truly be yourself with another it supersedes everything. At the heart of all this of course is trust, which sits at the core of every happy ever after I have personally ever witnessed.

Listen you are only human and there will be bumps along the way, so don't get bogged down in panicking about this, that and the other. Going with the flow and enjoying life, remembering to celebrate it and treasure what you have is far more important than anything in your quest for happiness. Live today, don't wait for tomorrow is my motto and a philosophy that should also be at the heart of any successful relationship. As much as this book is about taking steps to prevent and manage situations effectively that pop up along the way, I don't want you questioning and analysing every twist and turn. Learning to go with the flow by not over-thinking and letting life just evolve, is as much a skill to master as any other in this mission to happily ever after.

As I say, my only key point of caution is that men can easily turn into idle creatures if given half a chance and I definitely do not want you wallowing in such an existence. Once a month or every quarter, do something out of the ordinary. Break routines, rules and curfews. Go wild in the aisles. God damn it, rip all your clothes off and run down the street naked for all I care. Life is supposed to be an adventure after all and I am not just talking about the annual summer holiday! Life, love and laughter are my three favourite words in the World and making the most of them in equal measure is your ultimate key to happiness. This is no dress rehearsal lady. Rock every day as if it were your last. And that means from today – whether you have bagged a bloke yet or not! Remember a positive you on the inside Radiates on the outside.

Look at any successful relationship and you will always find the woman on top and in control. Men love and thrive on that sense of domination on a day to day basis. Yes it does require a little confidence within on your part, but that will evolve naturally when you are the adored rather than the adorer. One should always sit in the seat of the former, leading, instructing and guiding from the front. You, in reality, are the true master in moulding and shaping this happy ever after. Men need it. They may think they are in charge, but that couldn't be further from the truth. Even beyond the mundane of day to day existence, take the driving seat, drop a nugget in the ocean and watch him run with it. Let him think he dreamt up the holiday of a lifetime or found the new set of wheels you've had your eye on for weeks. Men love nothing more than believing they have just conjured up the greatest idea ever known to man in an attempt to impress you. But subconsciously of course, the ball is firmly in your court without him even realising it. I know it all sounds a little manipulating, but what can I say? Welcome to the World of lifelong happiness darling! The trick is to make him feel like a Prince, but really, you are King.

I must admit, as I take a moment to read this little lot back, I am not even sure myself as to whether I am promoting lifelong happiness here at times or a life sentence! But like any decent military operation, this book is about arming you with all the necessary tools for a blissful existence and that means we need to sometimes cover uncomfortable ground. Don't ignore the obvious and never shy away from a difficult conversation. Ignorance is never bliss. Confront and comfort, may have opposite meanings, but they are words of equal measure. Confront where you need to and support whenever you can. Only secrets and lies breed barriers. Face such obstacles before the three vital components of trust, honesty and openness start to fade away. Once that happens it's a long road back to where you first started. Yes honesty really is always the best policy. And laughter is the greatest medicine of them all. As is never going to bed on an argument unresolved. I guess a true love that holds no boundaries whatsoever is the ultimate existence after all.

Every happy ever after has its challenges for sure, but remember, the 'L' word always prevails in the end and will light up even the darkest of tunnels. All you need is love! Love conquers all. Love lifts us up where we belong. Love changes everything! And if it's full throttle, nothing will ever stop it.

Dealing with the Mother-in-Law

Kill her with kindness, be patient, respectful, and never give her a reason to make you an enemy.

Now this is most definitely a chapter for the back pocket! And in my own experiences from the wedding World, the Mother-in-Law on either side can often prove to be a very tricky beast to tame. In this chapter we shall cover the most extreme of the species. For a girl who fails to prepare is prepared to fail. I am not purposely trying to whip you up into an unnecessary frenzy here – I am sure one's M-I-L is going to be utterly glorious and everything you ever dreamt of – it's just a case of me being me and preparing you for the worst case scenario. Oh and of course for pure entertainment value too! I always find a good laugh takes the edge off any challenging situation and dealing with the M-I-L is definitely no exception.

In a nutshell, you do just essentially need to get her on side – AKA do whatever it takes for the woman to like you. Win her over whole-heartedly with not a behind the back jab or bitchy throwaway comment in sight and you'll be home and dry. So remember, first impressions really do count. Always dress to impress and put your best foot forward at all times. An effort on your part shows you care and I can guarantee you the Mother-in-Law cares – even if she doesn't display it. In the same vein, show solidarity and support in her opinions and NEVER work against her. This is a dangerous game to play. Ultimately your husband-to-be will want you to get on. That is the end game here, so don't give yourself unnecessary headaches. Just smile and move on if you feel a confrontation brewing. And yes, when in the midst of a whirlwind romance it is difficult to think about much else, but the M-I-L is one such creature you should never ignore or ever be complacent about. Taking your eye off the ball with this one could heavily impact on your mental health, not to mention the general well-being of your relationship further down the line, so let's sit back, relax and break this thing down…

First impressions really do count BIG TIME with the M-I-L and it's good to be a little nervous and show some vulnerability in the beginning too, let her feel like a powerhouse you are mildly in awe of. Keen to please but never desperate, any whiff of desperation and you've had it. Desperation in her eyes could translate into unstable and she isn't going to want that for her little Prince Charming Darling now is she? As in life, it's all about getting the balance right. On your third meeting suggest a lunch or shopping trip together – bond with her even if you don't want to. And anyway, stepping outside of your comfort zone every now and then is good for mind, body and soul. Everyone's a winner when it comes to dealing with the M-I-L – positive thinking remember!

Next up is what I call 'the filter and throw approach'… aka in one ear and out the other. Take her ideas on board and seem interested even if you couldn't care less. I am pretty sure she will have some mildly over-bearing opinions to impart on how you should rock the wedding or bring the kids up, but again just filter and throw. To be fair, some of them you may end up agreeing with – shock horror! Acknowledge her knowledge, even integrate a little something every now and then to show willing – just don't ever dismiss her. Nobody likes to be dismissed, or made to feel like their opinion doesn't matter. Always thank your M-I-L for all the valuable wisdom she has kindly shared and make it clear that you will reflect on everything she says – make her feel special, but obviously don't patronise. And remember she is the one losing a little something from her life and you are the one gaining everything... from her! When or if it's ever your turn, I am sure you will feel her pain too, so be gentle. Life is but a cycle of repetitions and cyclical movements after all. Trust me, you will think back and reflect on this read in twenty years time and a moment of empathy will prevail if you have your own kids.

It's also important to avoid confrontation at all costs. If you feel a conversation is heating up slightly, just kill it. And if it's a situation that needs revisiting, simply say you have 'both' come to a decision on said issue – planning something for the wedding for example. She has very limited room for manoeuvre then if her little soldier is standing by you. Yes she might have done the wedding before and successfully raised a pack of little ones blah blah blah, but that doesn't mean it's her way or the highway. Anyway don't bother going down that road, this is all simply an exercise in people management – a skill for life and who better than the M-I-L to perfect your technique on!

In general, couples tend to gravitate more towards the female's family and that can leave your new Mother-in-Law-to-be feeling a bit left out, isolated and vulnerable. Be sensitive of that fact. Obviously as a total Princess the focus is always going to be on you and your World and why the hell not! But this is often why barriers start to build in the first place. And when you think about it, who is she going to take it all out on – you if you're not careful. Show her that you are keen to build an inclusive family unit and her voice counts. Listen, let's break it down. The poor cow is finding it difficult to let go, desperately clinging on to her boy for dear life. Work to make her trust you and realise he is in safe hands.

Now she may well prove to be a tough cookie to crack at first, but if you play the long game and keep persevering, she will indeed crack, if not melt like putty in your hands for you to shape and sculpt as you so desire. The M-I-L can be anything and everything, from a bit clucky, right through to a hardcore possessive. Brace yourself for every possible outcome, but prey for the former! And if in doubt, as I say, just kill her with kindness. That old chestnut never fails. If you play it all sweetness and light where can she go with all that bitterness and angst? Absolutely nowhere is the answer. The M-I-L will be left out in the cold by all those around her if she does attempt an attack and I guarantee, Mother dearest will certainly not won't that! Just make sure you steer clear of any reverse psychology tactics or trying to play her at her own game. Remember she's an expert and will catch you out, or at worse turn members of her inner circle against you, which could kick off all manner of uncomfortable confrontations.

Riding that theme, don't ever be tempted to go bad mouthing the M-I-L to your Mr Right either. Even if armed with solid evidence that the two-faced Witch is bitching about you behind your back. It's a rookie error so many make. Not only does it place him slap bang in the middle of a difficult situation, it also starts to create barriers that can be difficult to breakdown. And not only with your M-I-L, but also with your partner feeling resentful for the tension you may be seen as having created. He might not show it, but internally he will be pained by such conversations and in turn that is going to affect and impact on you. Why cause yourself a headache – take the easy life option I say. Even if you hate her, don't spite her because it will come back to haunt you.

I guess this philosophy applies to your life together in general. Avoid all unnecessary confrontation and let frustrations with all external relationships wash over your head to minimise stress levels. Most importantly though, never ever make him choose between you and the M-I-L. Ultimatums are never sexy and tend to turn off instead of turn on. The M-I-L is never a threat to what you can offer, so take a reality check and move on girl if you start going down such a path. Life is about different relationships fulfilling different roles. The M-I-L for example has an unconditional love you simply cannot match, whilst at the same time your 'in-love' cannot be touched either. Accept such differences in life and move on. Jealousy is a killer.

Ironically, you may end up annoying each other a little because you might actually be pretty similar in character. I do strongly believe that guys are drawn to characteristics they know, love and understand. If you don't click, this is probably why. You are too similar! Remember this point, keep it in your back pocket and react accordingly – or don't react as the case may be if she winds you up. And I don't mean in a weird, freaky, in-bred, he fancies his Mum type way, just elements of her that he loves and looks for in a girl. Unless of course he hates her too and then it's a totally different story! Just remember in general, there is much to learn about your partner by observing the M-I-L in action because she is the one that has shaped him in the first place. As I say, work with her not against her.

And if she does upset you every now and then, don't let it dominate the rest of your life. Forgive, forget and move on. At the same time if she genuinely is a total nagging nightmare for you both, don't pull him away from her, let him realise on his own terms and navigate his desired path gradually. A tiny piece of him will hate you if you try, or are seen to be sabotaging their bond by others. Let such a situation evolve just as nature intended. Your Prince will always come back to you in the end no matter what, because you are his future.

I guess staying on that theme – the only problematic ones are the Mummy's boys. So protected, shielded, pampered and downright smothered that you cannot get a look in. It begs the question as to whether this is the kind of Prince you are looking for in the first place really? Sounds like a lifetime of bloody hard work to me. Yes, all guys should have a special love and protection for said M-I-L, but if he's like a man possessed, well, we have a big problem that only a sizeable bout of therapy could cure. Best to uncover these worst case scenarios during the early days if you ask me, because if you think it's bad pre-wedding, imagine having to deal with an over-bearing Grandmother on a daily basis?! And if his Mum's not around, look out for the M-I-L in disguise. A special protector that can often be worse! Investigate, infiltrate and take the appropriate action.

As I say, we are dealing with the most extreme cases here because it would be dull not too. I am sure your M-I-L-to-be will embrace you with open arms, a slice of carrot cake in one hand and a skinny latte in the other. Or at the very worst, be a watered down version of the nightmares discussed above! I am of course joking. To be fair, she'll probably be thrilled by the chance to offload an offspring. Delighted that her boy has finally found that extra special someone he loves and adores and vice versa. Surely that is all any Mother worth her weight in gold would desire? These are the M-I-L's to cherish. Not only will she play a pivotal role in strengthening and supporting your relationship going forward, she will also become a friend for life too. Someone to rely on, turn to for advice and an all-round ally really, because she will know how you're Prince-in-waiting operates better than anyone and that kind of insight is truly priceless.

And remember – you're his lover not his mother!

I repeat, ALWAYS remember, you are his lover not his mother! If you let that shift in dynamic take hold, it's very difficult to reverse and before you know it, one has subconsciously morphed into the Mother-in-Law. And that is not a role any lover should aspire too! You are not his carer or comfort blanket, you are his lover darling. His partner yes, and potentially Mother to his kids – but not him. Yes it's true, for whatever reason, all guys love a little mothering every now and then, but such a dynamic can easily spiral out of control if not managed correctly. I am sure some Freudian theory could sum it all up nicely about why men like to be smothered, but signing up to be head cook and bottle washer, pandering to his every need and whim is not on my agenda here. Let him wash and iron his own shirts – it is the 21st century after all.

Men spend 90% of their adult lives with just one thing on the brain and that definitely doesn't involve an apron or a pair of rubber gloves. To put it bluntly, sex should be at the heart of any healthy relationship and never should it be relegated to second position as the day to day of life and household routine takes hold. Don't get me wrong, I am not asking you to give it away like a big of chips every five minutes. If anything you really must treat him mean to keep him keen as the saying goes. There is of course a reason why all men love bitches! The endless chase, the addictive thrill and the buzz of it all is what makes life interesting. What we are talking about here is being cautious of the subtle switch from Lover to Mother that can easily evolve and take hold if you let it. In fact, most of the time it happens to couples without them even realising. Be conscious of such a potential shift happening in the first place and put a stop to it.

Obsessing over perfecting his minor imperfections, finishing his sentences, issuing any form of instruction – or at worse, telling him off like a naughty schoolchild are all symptoms to steer clear of. I am slightly joking here of course, but check out some of your friends in a long-term relationship. It's unbelievable how this process can organically just 'happen' over time without either party realising. If not careful – before you know it – you become that bossy bore you always dreaded morphing in to, and it's not even your fault, because you were never warned of such a transformation until now. I once witnessed a girlfriend issuing a very well thought-out step-by-step guide to cleaning the fridge for her other half to follow. Utterly hilarious and if you'd filmed it, I am convinced the video would have gone viral. Yes guys love to be bossed around a bit, but taking on the role of school matron is not a sexy move.

Technically of course, women are mentally more advanced than men, thinking first and acting second. Herein lies you're problem. As I said at the top of this book, I am often perplexed by the fact a man can walk into a bar full of strippers and have the time of his life without a single thought or care for the performer's situation. A woman on the other hand would think about why they were doing such a job, how they must feel and what a desperate state they must be in. The only time a man would care is if his own daughter was up there doing it?! A black and white thought process with little depth for analysis. In some ways this is a blessing I guess, but it does mean that women in general tend to take way more than their fair share of the mental stresses and strains of life onto their shoulders – especially when the family starts growing!

Don't feel obliged to take charge of the day-to-day, because before you know it, he will just sit back, relax, enjoy the ride, and do approximately zilch – whilst allowing you to carry the load. Think back to your childhood, I bet your mother headed up the planning of literally everything. The big summer holiday and Sunday afternoon daytrip probably not so bad, but managing the household every day must have been a bit of a misery and mildly relentless at times. I actually remember thinking that myself. But the point is you don't have too. Men love to be tasked with duties as we have discussed previously, in fact they thrive on it. And yes you may well be raging inside, desperate to do things your way because you know it's better – any women worth her weight in gold would do the same – but you need to hold back and let him take the lead in your day to day lives every now and then also, firstly to ensure you don't cross that all important boundary into Mother not lover territory, and secondly because he is perfectly capable.

Remember one should never be taken for granted either, otherwise life can easily become a bit of a slog if you're not careful.

And anyway, the more mistakes he makes the better, because you will be waiting in the wings ready to pick up the pieces, once again reiterating how utterly fabulous you really are and what a lucky boy he is to have you in the first place. Everyone's a winner! And make mistakes he will, but don't hold him to ransom over them. Actually a little healthy competition between you both is a good thing. Keeps you on your toes and your Prince always striving to do better! The unfortunate newsflash and bigger picture here of course, is that even a Prince among Men will make mistakes based on this statement. Damn it! I wanted utter perfection. Turns out even a wedding fairy can get it wrong every now and then. Oh and on that note, do also remember that even the finest of the male species can get a little tipsy on occasion, but don't judge like you really are his Mother… unless of course he throws up on your favourite jumper! Then quite clearly you have every right to be angry verging upon livid. How dare he? Took me quite a while to whip up that line of rhyming poetic genius FYI!

Fundamentally what I am saying here is let the M-I-L deal with all the pandering & Mothering and you just focus on the love-making. The roles should have clear distinction and not filter into one. You started out as lovers and it should stay that way. Many may disagree arguing there is some cross over, but conscious boundaries should always be drawn before it's too late. All healthy relationships start by sharing and experiencing equally together. Don't ever let that philosophy for life disintegrate. The emphasis of course is on the 'sharing' not instructing, otherwise again, if you're not careful within 10 years you will be bogged down in managing what he does, says, eats and thinks. You mustn't allow the dynamic of where the partnership started dissolve into a watered down version, or indeed something incomprehensively different and unrecognisable. I am always a little disturbed when 'the other half' is also described as a 'best friend'. They are not your best friend! They are however, your lover, partner and soul-mate for life. At least that is what we are aiming for as discussed throughout this entire book! And you are not and never should be a partner's Mother figure. Keep conscious of this fact. Evolution is not always a good thing if you take a wrong turn you could have easily avoided folks.

Life is for living, it really is very precious and your whole World could easily be turned upside down in an instant. Don't spend a day in a job you hate, or at war with a friend or family member. Regret is a terrible thing. Work to enjoy and treasure every second of every day from this point forward, because tomorrow may be a day that never comes… and as another dear friend always says to me, you never see a safe following a hearse, so eat, drink and be merry!

And Finally...

81 things every girl must know about the male species by REAL people who know!

As a little finale, I commissioned a survey into what real people think you should know about men. Wise words to reflect upon in places and others quite hilarious responses in my opinion! But hey, everything in life is in the eye of the beholder so go judge for yourself. It's always quite tricky when you ask such a question that the whole thing doesn't just turn into a man bashing session. A bit like when you go to a restaurant, we rarely take the time to write or comment about how amazing it was – only if was rubbish! Fingers crossed though, it's all come together as a rounded lovely gathering of words with a few thoughts from me thrown in for good measure too.

Responses have been kept anonymous, but ironically, after everything discussed in this book, I would say that the guy's comments are generally a bit lighter on the content/depth front... see if you can spot them!

If a woman asks, 'what are you thinking about?'... It's probably football.
G: The depths of an average male psyche officially confirmed.

Men think 'will I get caught'... women think 'can I live with myself'.
G: Obviously the sub-text to this one is certainly not something for us to dwell on.

All men are a little bit gay.
G: Only a homosexual could say/wish this me thinks. Ten pints in maybe!

Most men DO NOT wash their hands after going to the toilet.
G: Horrifyingly as previously discussed, I can indeed confirm this. Gross I know.

Always look at a girl, if she can't look after herself, how the hell is she ever going to be able to look after me?
G: Another interesting insight and as ever, it's all about him! Bloody attention seekers. Mother's have so much to answer for and Freud for that matter – clearly spoilt rotten this one.

Men like sex!
G: I don't think anyone would argue with that drunken statement girlfriend.

All men are fickle as a fish.
G: Isn't everyone at times?

The only man ever worth talking to is the one who is prepared to adore not have to be adored.
G: Heavy words with a heavy sentiment, but you know what, this says it all in one sentence and something I have mentioned many times in my book… could this possibly be my own hidden quote?! Keep an eye out, who knows there could be more – move over Banksy!

If he's not talking about sex, he's most definitely thinking about it.
G: Fact.

A real man won't judge your drunken behaviour and will always be there to nurse your hangover.
G: I wouldn't push the boundaries too far on that one love. I mean, chucking your guts up whilst pissing your knickers is not ideal for either party.

Mr Right will always make you feel comfortable in your own skin.
G: So true.

Judge every Man by the way he treats his Mother.
G: Or any of those near and dear to him. We certainly would not like to discriminate here… his Mother might be a total cow!

Don't try to change him – he won't change… accept that and you've cracked it.
G: Wise words, proper wise words.

Steer clear of damaged goods.
G: Wow, harsh words! A guy with an unsettled past can be challenging I won't lie, but anything is fixable I guess if the connection is right?

Men are so much easier to work with than women.
G: Sounds like there is more to this one than meets the eye…

The male species are stunted emotionally and I am actually rather jealous of that fact!
G: Yep in general, men are pretty black and white in their thought processes, whereas the average women will consider a million grey areas.

Men love an organised existence.
G: Depends on the man surely?

What you see is what you get.
G: Not always love.

Most Men are fundamentally just attention seekers.
G: indeed.

Guys just want to have fun.
G: Who doesn't?

We're generally more adventurous and not so concerned with the consequences, whereas women tend to be a little bit more cautious about everything.
G: Throw caution to the wind and walk with open abandonment if you are on board with this statement. Personally I am not sure if we should totally take this one to heart, a guy who is not bothered about consequences is one to steer clear of in my opinion – for all the obvious reasons.

A real keeper is the one who doesn't change.
G: I think by this she means around his mates. You know how some guys can play up and act like total knobs around their pals, almost morphing into a completely different person? Yeah I am on board with that comment.

Recognise early on if his primary goal is to please you… if so, never let him go because in most circumstances that will last until the day he dies.
G: As I always say, a lot can be said for the classic people pleaser in love and one thing is for sure, they are generally very reliable and totally genuine.

Ambition is a total turn on.
G: Isn't that applicable for both sexes? And not just limited to career aspirations. Ambitions for marriage, a family and a home can all be turn-ons, just depends which one or mix floats your boat. Ambitions must be mutual. This is one area where opposites do not attract.

Men are less complicated than women.
G: I would disagree. Many just try to hide their complications, which is half the battle in unravelling them.

Men are like a dog chasing a bone – just make sure he never finds it.
G: Nice analogy.

Don't think you can ever cure a player, you can't. Period.
G: Like attempting to change someone's sexuality... it just isn't going to happen.

If you are not his sole primary focus, ditch him.
G: Healthy to have other interests, but you must be priority number one.

Men operate like a pack of wolves, in a group they are domineering and powerful, on their own they can be vulnerable and weak.
G: Proper little nugget of wisdom this one.

Guys like to think they are in control and on top.
G: Let them I say, we all know who's in the driving seat really. Why flatten their ego? I suspect it will actually make them feel more confident within the relationship in the long run anyhow.

Never try and belittle or make a guy feel inferior or stupid. It's what makes them want to cheat in the first place.
G: Controversial words here. But one thing is for sure, if a guy does cheat, it is NEVER your fault.

Men cheat because they get bored.
G: Only boring people get bored. Every one of us should take responsibility for our own actions.

Some guys are just genetically wired to cheat.
G: Do you know what, I actually agree. I think some people (not just men) are turned on by the thrill of it all. Fingers crossed we don't meet any of them hey!

Most men have a very short attention span.
G: And cannot multi-task to save their lives, as many of us have first-hand experience of.

Men never ever get bored of sex.
G: Again, is that not the case for both sexes? Don't try and play it all innocent with me girl. I know exactly who wrote this comment and trust me, *plain-Jane-no-nonsense* she is not! To be fair, it does depend on how you decide to interpret this one – perhaps they are both at it like rabbits and she's talking from experience? Who knows, people can sometimes say one thing and mean something completely different.

Actually, most guys just want to provide!
G: Hallelujah! Praise the Lord. There are some Prince's left out there.

The majority of blokes take their responsibilities very seriously and are totally committed.
G: #feelingeuphoric

If he truly loves you, he cannot live without you.
G: #speechless

A REAL man would choose you over the footie!
G: I am going to stop with the hash-tag thing now before it gets really annoying. This is a joke right? I am not convinced... :) instead this time!!

Men are quite happy to just go with the flow, don't beat him up over it.
G: Yes, but some men are masters of 'staying quiet' – don't let him get away with that either. 'Anything for an easy life' is how I believe the saying goes. Yeah right – not on my watch mate! Why should you take the weight of the World onto your shoulders, whilst he sits back and enjoys the ride?

Men are less curious and less interested than women.
G: Oh please, guys love a good bitch every now and then. And I don't just mean the gay ones!

If he says he's not interested in marriage dump him.
G: As I mentioned in a previous chapter, the amount of times I've read or heard about a 10 year relationship finishing, only for one to run off, meet the person of their dreams and then announce after 6 months they are getting hitched is utterly ridiculous. And again, it's not that I think marriage is the be all and end all, it's just if someone is adamant they don't ever want to get married, it makes me wonder why? What is the big problem with that level of commitment if you've unearthed a soul mate? Or is it more to do with the fact that deep down inside they know the relationship is not for them in the long term?

The male sex has an amazing ability to just switch off, don't take it personally.
G: And a very limited attention span too.

Women love to argue, men prefer a quiet life.
G: Not always, but most of the time I think you are probably right here.

Women over-think things, men rarely do.
G: Fact.

Guys tend to just let things go, whereas women hold a grudge – for a lifetime.
G: Sounds like this guy has first-hand experience and probably deservedly so.

Men repeat their jokes.
G: Surely that's the joy of a 'Dad joke' in the first place? Especially at Christmas!

All men need a hobby.
G: Keeps the grey matter ticking over… particularly for the older gentlemen.

It's not all about the physical you know, men need mental stimulation too!
G: Of course they do.

Sport is the only other relationship in a man's life that matters.
G: What about the kids?!

But men just don't have the listening abilities of women.
G: Enough is enough. I need some positivity back into my life right now. At this rate the only place you'll be heading is the local lesbian singles night!

The majority of blokes would die for their family.
G: And there you go. This gorgeous statement separates the men from the boy's right? Sacrifice on any level is the ultimate commitment I think and aphrodisiac for that matter too.

Believe it or not, when it comes to it, men will fight for what they believe in.
G: Oh yes we are cooking on gas people's!

Most blokes are shite at DIY
G: Or deluded about their skill base, either way, most really are shite at DIY.

I think we are all gagging to have a go in the kitchen.
G: Yes even though the food combinations may be a little experimental at times, let him attempt a culinary masterpiece on high days and holidays. Practice makes perfect as they say. If all else fails, give him a few staples and recipes to work from… sausage surprise anyone? What a mildly sexist statement this one is too!

The garden is a man's domain.
G: Alright, calm down Godzilla. I guess the kitchen sink is a woman's right? This is the 21st century people share and share alike... including household duties!

It's a man's job to put out the bins.
G: I cannot imagine many women arguing with that statement.

Women cannot iron shirts as well as men.
G: I feel a challenge coming on...

Men are hypochondriacs.
G: This is true, especially post hangover. It may surprise you, but I myself am a total drama Queen when it comes to diagnosing emerging ailments.

Men are obsessed with their penises.
G: From a young age I believe.

Man flu does exist.
G: Really? I think not.

Old men are grumpy gits by nature.
G: And rather endearing too in my opinion. A man in his later years that has lived never fails to be fascinating.

A pensive man is the most interesting to know.
G: Or the biggest challenge?

No matter what the age, for some reason, they love nothing more than to fart.
G: Who doesn't love a spot of oral or anal every now and then? Flatulence rocks its official. And the more bombastic the better I think. Be loud and proud people... although maybe leave it a while before you let one rip in front of your new potential Prince and definitely NOT in a public setting!

Guys are not really that bothered about anything outside of their own lives.

G: True men can become a little insular and enwrapped in their own little world, which isn't necessarily a bad thing. You just need to make sure you both step outside of it every now and then to keep things fresh and interesting.

Men are as tight as a ducks arse!

G: As in tight on the financials? Such a West Country expression! And surely not true in all cases?

A good man is always first up to the bar.

G: I'll raise a glass to that one – cheers!

If he's quiet it doesn't mean he is shy, he's probably quietly confident.

G: It's not always the loudest voice in the room that gets the most attention…

The loudest voice in the room is quite often the hardest to have a relationship with.

G: Nice link from one quote to another I thought!

Men love it when you laugh at their jokes.

G: Who doesn't?! My friend says I stole his personality when it comes to comedy. How very rude, I simply make his jokes sound much better.

Nobody's perfect.

G: Amen.

The one's that love themselves will never love you enough.

G: Vanity is a tough one to compete with.

A bully is broken inside.

G: Sad but true.

Men are so competitive, they hate to be beaten.
G: I know some pretty competitive Ladies too!

Jealousy is an aphrodisiac.
G: A new one on me? Does it work for you?

A man can be surprisingly caring when needed to step up to the mark.
G: Thanks goodness.

They like to experiment!
G: Not quite sure what this particular sound-bite was all about, will leave to your imagination. I was too scared to indulge further.

At the end of the day the majority are decent.
G: Sounds a little dull, but I just had to pop this one in for my own sanity after writing this book.

Confidence is the biggest turn-on.
G: Based on the conversations I've had with pretty much every girl I know, I would tend to agree with you.

If you think he's talking shit, he most definitely is.
G: An insightful and profound statement, so eloquently put.

Most guys genuinely just want the same thing as you...
G: Love. It's what every human vessel was built for.

Acknowledgements and Thoughts

Right I need a drink! Wow, writing this book was like analysing a potential blue-print for the perfect existence. And it turns out – when intoxicated – most people are pretty convinced they hold the secret formula, and I have very much enjoyed reflecting on each and every one of those wise words over the past 3 years or so (on and off whilst working on this little number) – which has of course culminated in this hilarious, laugh out loud, show-stopping read. Not that I am trying to control your psyche or anything, but if you say something often enough, it turns out people really do start to believe it right? A genuine analysis on this piece of literary genius is all I ask for. See what I did there? Clever I know. Look into my eyes, look into my eyes, not around the eyes... look into my eyes – and you're under. Whipping out the crystal ball and DIY hypnosis kit as we speak for a positive outcome on the reviews front!

Talking of drinks, I must firstly turn my attentions to the rather fabulous drunken contributions and all the very lovely people who gave a little piece of their soul to this read. And yes, I love you too. I really do! Don't you just adore the insightful head of an intoxicated deep and meaningful? To be fair, some pretty great content came out of a few of those sessions, so perhaps there really is something to be said about being able to achieve World Peace courtesy of that finale double vodka and coke? It's always one more for the road with my lot, but in my experience it rarely is. Perhaps it was that crossing of the border between tipsy and shit-faced I sourced my greatest words of wisdom and nuggets of knowledge only life-experience itself can teach. Whatever it was, I thank you friends and family alike for being such wise old owls and inspiring my next chapter.

Now in most cases, I suspect you have probably read this book because you are feeling a little flat when it comes to the dating scene. Tons of anxieties can start kicking-in when focused on finding Mr Right – especially when it's all basically going wrong! Now is the time to wipe all that away, reboot and start again. I cannot profess to being an expert in this field, just a wedding fairy with an opinion and a few observations after nearly a decade in the business of celebrating love, which I truly hope has given you food for thought. Having studied this subject matter for over 3 years, I also hope my book has not only entertained, but also given you the confidence boost that is sometimes needed to get back out there, re-energised and ready to hunt out a little love again. Honestly, it's been an education for me too!

Bizarrely I am not actually a massive reader of books myself –unless it's a biography from someone I am interested in – and even then it has to grab me pretty quickly. Patience is not a quality I possess in abundance and it is for this very reason, most of my friends are utterly gobsmacked I managed to finish writing this in the first place – let alone read it back and bother to edit it. And in all honestly, I have surprised myself too based on the general sphere of my attention span, which is annoyingly rather limited. Constantly amending, re-writing, adjusting and adding-to what started off as a blank piece of paper has been mentally exhausting! Much more so than I initially expected! It's been a labour of love on and off for quite some time. They say everybody has a book in them. Be that as it may, you need the patience of a saint to make it to the end without turning to drink. But I guess being naturally intrigued by the often curious behaviour of us humans has ultimately kept me on track and

I guess kept me interested in reaching an end point to this huge personal challenge.

And although I clearly set myself up for this by writing such a title, being asked to sum up the secret to finding Mr Right in just one sentence feels like an impossible question to answer now. Such a conversation – with any depth to it – could go on for hours. I guess if push comes to shove, I would start by telling people to be open to all possibilities, but if that all important *intrigue* does kick-in, pushing you forward to find out more about the man before you upon a first meet, well, it's likely you are on to something pretty exciting. A real fascination or curiosity in someone you have just met is an emotion rarely unearthed and supersedes everything in the long run – even an initial lust – although I guess you could argue the two are connected. See? I told you… we could go on for hours! Sometimes we do just have to accept there really isn't a singular answer to everything, just a bunch of ideas and thoughts we can all share with each other. The more complex a situation, the trickier it is to sum up. I guess the power of writing for me is in the learning, or to just remind ourselves that there isn't always a right or wrong way to do things, just a million possibilities… for life and love.

Having said all that, this is the very first time I have written outside of my wedding planning bubble and although a little daunting at first, I have genuinely loved every minute of it and really immersed myself in the process. I mean what's not to *love* about my chosen subject matter. It's all we need right? And being The Wedding Fairy, I guess sharing my recipe for success was the next obvious step. In a professional sense, I have uncovered the lot, from the guy who needs a little work, right through to the perfect gent who rarely puts a foot wrong. To think I wouldn't be able to impart such priceless knowledge with you just seemed like such a travesty! I actually surprised myself half the time by what I had subconsciously stored in my head on this particular subject matter. It's not until you sit down, reflect and write about something, that you realise how much you have learnt. So much so that I will definitely utilise in my own love life too!

And on that finishing note, I must also thank my publishers AUK and Oak Tree Press for giving me this opportunity and outlet to write in the first place, alongside my agency SLM for their continued support. If I look back now, I am so incredibly proud of what that blank word doc has turned in to. And the idea that a romance could spark from these here pages, is just ridiculous and exciting and fabulous beyond words! Who'd have thought a boy from the Mead Vale estate in Weston-super-Mare – who could barely read or write at 10 – would bang out a book. Turns out, a great teacher truly is the biggest blessing that is often taken for granted, life changing actually. Thank you so much Miss Collette for persevering with me, you saw a potential I didn't even know existed and for that I am eternally grateful. I hope one day I will be able to find you and thank you in person. And finally, to my lovely Mum for pushing me to open a book in the first place! It was a challenge my love, but we got there in the end.

George x

Whoever he is and wherever he may be waiting…
your Mr Right is out there somewhere.

Now is the time to go find him.

For when you have found Mr Right...

THE WEDDING FAIRY'S
BIG DAY
BREAKDOWN
PLANNING FOR AN UNFORGETTABLE CELEBRATION

George Watts

GEORGE WATTS, THE WEDDING FAIRY
AS SEEN ON TV!

Lightning Source UK Ltd.
Milton Keynes UK
UKOW02f1626141216
289984UK00001B/19/P